LEFT, RIGHT
&
BABYBOOM

LEFT, RIGHT & BABYBOOM

America's New Politics

edited by David Boaz

CATO
INSTITUTE

Library of Congress Cataloging in Publication Data

Left, right, and babyboom.

   1. Political science—United States—Addresses,
essays, lectures.   2. United States—Politics and
government—1981–   —Addresses, essays, lectures.
   I. Boaz, David, 1953–   . II. Title: Left, right,
and baby boom.
JA84.U5L38 1986   320.5′0973   86-2248
ISBN 0-932790-57-7

Printed in the United States of America.

CATO INSTITUTE
224 Second Street SE
Washington, D.C. 20003

Contents

Introduction

David Boaz

The magnitude of President Reagan's victory in 1984 obscured some important underlying political trends. While it is true that it is difficult to defeat an incumbent president during a time of peace and prosperity, it is also true that Americans did not by any means all support President Reagan for the same reasons.

Between now and 1988 there will be millions of words written about the post-Reagan political world. In this volume several leading political observers try to focus our attention on the key issues. In April 1985 the Cato Institute gathered these analysts together at a conference entitled "Reassessing the Political Spectrum." The results of that conference are presented here.

It is difficult to analyze any problem unless our language is adequate to convey a proper understanding of the issues under discussion. A reliance on inadequate language has hampered American political analysis for the last two decades. As Professors William S. Maddox and Stuart A. Lilie pointed out in their 1984 book, *Beyond Liberal and Conservative: Reassessing the Political Spectrum,* "The liberal-conservative dichotomy is inadequate to describe and understand the opinions and behavior of the American public."

Maddox and Lilie argued then, as they do in chapter 4 of this book, that many Americans cannot be rightly classified as either liberal or conservative. Yet this does not mean, as political scientists have traditionally assumed, that their political views are therefore "inconsistent" or "confused." There are consistent threads running through their beliefs that simply can't be categorized on the traditional political spectrum.

While we usually assume that we can place most voters and politicians on the liberal-conservative spectrum, a number of events in the past few years have seemed to undermine that assumption:
- The Scoop Jackson wing of the Democratic party was often described as conservative, yet it was clearly liberal on most economic issues.

1

- "Moderate" Democrats and "moderate" Republicans often receive similar scores on ideological ratings of congressional votes, yet their actual voting patterns may be strikingly different. Typically, moderate Republicans have a relatively conservative record on economic issues and a relatively liberal record on social and foreign policy issues, while moderate Democrats often have records that are just the opposite.
- John Anderson in 1980 and Gary Hart in 1984 seemed to appeal to younger voters with a unique combination of fiscal conservatism, social liberalism, and dovishness.
- Voters themselves frequently seem to defy categorization, as in recent national polls that have shown overwhelming support for both a nuclear freeze and a constitutional amendment to balance the federal budget.

What all these politicians and poll results have in common is that they cannot be neatly categorized on the traditional political spectrum. Maddox and Lilie offered one fundamental critique of the liberal-conservative approach. Their argument seemed obvious after it was explained, yet it had eluded political scientists, pollsters, and journalists for decades.

Maddox and Lilie pointed out that political scientists (and, less formally, pollsters and journalists) had traditionally divided voters into the liberal and conservative camps on the basis of two questions: whether to expand or decrease government intervention in the economy, and whether to expand or decrease civil liberties or personal freedoms. A person who supported government economic activism and a strong defense of civil liberties was a "liberal"; someone who opposed economic intervention as well as the expansion of personal freedoms was a "conservative." But, Maddox and Lilie argued, the answers to these questions may be combined to form a total of *four*, not two, positions. Thus, a person might support economic intervention but oppose the expansion of personal freedoms, or he might oppose economic intervention while supporting personal freedoms. Standard political analysis defines these people as "inconsistent"; Maddox and Lilie describe them as "populists" and "libertarians" and demonstrate that there are just as many voters in those two camps as in the two traditional categories.

Perhaps nowhere is the inadequacy of the liberal-conservative spectrum more apparent than with the baby-boom generation. The 75 million Americans born between 1946 and 1964—or everyone born after 1940, to take Pat Caddell's more expansive definition—

are certainly not uniform in their thinking. Nevertheless, they do seem to share some experiences and perspectives that set them apart from older Americans. When their parents were growing up, government was the institution that ended the Depression and won World War II. In the baby boomers' lives, government fought a very unpopular war, a president resigned in disgrace, and government economic planning led to inflation, unemployment, and stagflation. Government didn't solve the great problems of our time; it caused them.

These experiences gave the baby boomers a much more skeptical view of government than their parents had. In addition, more members of this generation had enough education to be comfortable questioning the decisions of political leaders. This skeptical attitude showed up first, of course, in the Sixties when the most vocal members of the generation marched for civil rights and then against the war in Vietnam. A cultural revolution took place, too, first on campus and then throughout the country as young people began to question many of the rules that had seemed certain to their parents.

It has become a cliché to say that the baby boomers are fiscally conservative and socially liberal, but clichés are often founded on truth. Polls do show this generation to be more conservative on economic issues than older voters, while they retain the social liberalism—or tolerance, as Lee Atwater more accurately calls it—acquired during the Sixties. A growing number of analysts recognize this point, but this book may be the first to focus attention on its implications.

Confirmation of this thesis has continued since the April 1985 conference. Gregory B. Markus and M. Kent Jennings of the University of Michigan, in their continuing study of the high-school class of 1965, find the fiscally conservative/socially liberal strain particularly strong among the "yuppie" element of these oldest baby boomers (whom Markus and Jennings define as those with a college degree, a professional or managerial job, and a family income of $30,000 or more—some 15 percent of the group). They found that in 1973 the (future) yuppies in the class were more liberal than their classmates, but by 1982 they had become markedly more conservative on economic issues while remaining socially liberal. By 1982 the major political differences among the generation revolved around social issues, with the yuppies more liberal. Like many observers, Markus and Jennings attribute the growing economic conservatism of the yuppies largely to their high incomes and high-status occupations. It would seem, however, that the years from 1965 to 1982 offered ample opportunity for intellectual and practical disillusionment with government economic programs. Also, the best-educated generation in American history surely was influenced to some extent by the important critiques of macroeconomic planning, regulation, and the welfare state offered by such people as F. A. Hayek, Milton Friedman, Thomas Sowell, George Gilder, and Charles Murray.

Last August, *Fortune* magazine studied young corporate executives, finding that "baby-boom business leaders are taking a fresh look at politics. Neither consistent liberals nor conservatives, they oppose government intervention in both the economy and their personal lives." D. Quinn Mills, a Harvard Business School professor and author of a book on baby-boom executives called *The New Competitors*, estimates that 60 percent of young managers could be considered libertarian.

Pat Caddell has said recently that while 15 years ago the marginal voter in American politics was liberal on economics and conservative on social issues—perhaps the famous 47-year-old Dayton housewife married to a union member—today's marginal voter is just the opposite, economically conservative and socially liberal. This change will obviously have important implications for the political future.

The baby-boom generation first shook up American politics in the 1960s, when many of its members demanded an end to the war in Vietnam. Then as now, the baby boomers represented a new perspective, an alternative to politics-as-usual, that posed a problem for the political establishment. That establishment at first tried to ignore the young people who were demanding—in none-too-polite terms—an immediate end to the war. Then Sen. Eugene McCarthy gave them a political voice with his 1968 presidential campaign, as did Sen. George McGovern in 1972.

McCarthy and McGovern were established political figures, if not quite the establishment, so it may be that a similar figure will emerge to lead the new baby-boom movement. At least one thing is different today, however: the federal election laws make challenges to the establishment much more difficult. The McCarthy and McGovern campaigns would never have gotten off the ground without the contributions of hundreds of thousands of dollars from Stewart Mott, Max Palevsky, and other wealthy liberals. Today such con-

4

tributions would be illegal. The abuses of the Nixon fundraising operation in 1972 largely inspired the current election laws, yet the Reagan reelection campaign in 1984 should have proved that an incumbent Republican president can raise plenty of money legally. Nixon would not have been seriously hampered by a $1,000 limit on contributions, but the McGovern campaign would have been impossible. It is non-mainstream campaigns—which lack the advantages of incumbency, organization, or media recognition—that need large amounts of seed money. The election laws are thus a protective mechanism for the political establishment.

McCarthy and McGovern enfranchised a generation. They created a constituency for a new political idea, and they helped the country avoid an even more divisive social conflict by channeling popular outrage into the political process. Today, as always, there is a bias against change in the political establishment. Despite the growth of the baby-boom constituency, few members of Congress have made any serious efforts to respond to it. The recent centrist victories of Tom Kean in New Jersey and Gerald Baliles in Virginia are being touted as examples of fiscally conservative, socially liberal campaigns—yet neither Kean nor Baliles offers any prospect of real change.

The 1988 presidential campaign is a crucial test. Will a candidate emerge to appeal to the baby boomers in proposing change in a positive direction? Primaries, unfortunately, are not a good testing ground for a new idea: they tend to draw party activists who are unrepresentative of the general public. McCarthy and McGovern were able to bring a new group of voters into the Democratic primaries, but today Democratic primaries are dominated by AFL-CIO activists, Social Security recipients, and traditional liberals, not by a group receptive to new approaches and new ideas. Republican primaries likewise are dominated by older voters and staunch conservatives. Gary Hart tried to bring new voters into the Democratic primary process, but he did not widen the electorate enough.

Just as the baby boomers rebelled in the 1960s against old ways—what Hart calls "old arrangements"—so they may rebel in the 1980s and 1990s against the legacy of the past: against a Social Security system from the 1930s that costs them much and promises them little, against a military alliance system from the 1940s that now costs almost $200 billion a year to defend the wealthy countries of Europe and Asia, against the continuing attempts of the Republican right to reimpose the "family values" of the 1950s, against the failed

5

social programs of the 1960s. They may demand a new agenda of opportunity, tolerance, and peace, and we can only hope that our political system is not too rigidified to produce a candidate who has that agenda.

These questions and others are considered by the contributors to this volume. In chapter 1, William Schneider of the American Enterprise Institute argues that "all successful political innovation in this country is propelled by anti-establishment feeling." The Democrats' problem is that they managed to end up on the wrong side of that attitude: the country came to see them as the party of the federal government, and the federal government as the establishment. Schneider urges that Democrats find a way "to make the power of government once again seem populist rather than elitist."

Pollster Mervin Field describes his examination of the ideological views of Californians in light of Maddox and Lilie's four-way matrix. In a recent California Poll, he had asked respondents to describe themselves as liberal or conservative and to answer a number of questions on such issues as government-guaranteed jobs, Medicare, the draft, and regulation. By classifying people according to their positions on the key ideological issues, he found that a full third of Californians could be better described as libertarians or populists than as liberals or conservatives.

Dotty Lynch, pollster for the Gary Hart campaign, discusses the importance of the anti-establishment theme in the Democratic party's battles and chides the Mondale campaign for allowing itself to be portrayed as the establishment. She also examines "why the gender gap didn't happen"—why women gave a majority of their votes to President Reagan, and concludes that the Reagan campaign effectively convinced women—even young working women—that economic issues were more important than women's rights and that Reagan had a better program for the economy.

In the second chapter, "The Politics of the Baby Boom," Republican consultant Lee Atwater discusses the baby boom in cultural terms. He finds that the materialism of the 1950s, the new consciousness of the 1960s, and the "malaise" of the 1970s have led to "new values" today among the baby-boom generation—including self-actualization, quality, opportunity, tolerance, and social conscience, as well as a hostility to bigness in government, business, and other institutions.

I argue in this chapter that no presidential candidate has yet appeared to appeal to the fiscally conservative, socially liberal baby boomers. "The future of American politics," I conclude, "may be determined by whether the Democrats can liberate themselves from the grip of the AFL-CIO before the Republicans break free from the Moral Majority."

Democratic pollster Pat Caddell excoriates the Democratic party's "death wish to drive this generation away." He stresses the baby boomers' interest in social and political change, arguing, "The party that has been about change has always been the dominant party in this country." Caddell concludes that the party that gives the baby boomers an opportunity to act on their "collective social conscience" to effect positive change will be the majority party for the rest of the century.

Two young members of Congress who are at the center of their respective parties' efforts to come to grips with the new trends in politics offered their contrasting views at the conference's luncheon session. Rep. Vin Weber (R-Minn.) argues that "the old linkage of activist government–better times–Democrat is rapidly becoming less government–better times–Republican." He acknowledges a tension in the Republican party between evangelical Christians and the more libertarian younger voters but argues that the Republican program will manage to hold both groups and create a Republican majority.

Rep. Tim Wirth (D-Colo.) says that the political battle will be decided on the basis of two issues: who controls the center, and who defines the role of the federal government. The center of politics will be controlled, he suggests, by the party that combines the fundamental themes of opportunity and growth, or the Jeffersonian theme and the Hamiltonian theme. The role of government, he believes, is seen by most Americans not as a conflict between more and less government but as a question of how the public and private sectors can best work together.

In the fourth chapter of this volume, Stuart Lilie and William Maddox present the basic themes of their book *Beyond Liberal and Conservative*, namely, that a four-way, liberal-conservative-libertarian-populist analysis defines the American electorate much better than the traditional liberal-conservative spectrum. Lilie describes the historical roots of the four perspectives in American political thought, and Maddox discusses the implications of their analysis for future presidential politics.

Michael Barone of the *Washington Post* says that political observers will find the four-way matrix a useful tool for looking at politics.

For the time being, however, he thinks none of the four groups the categories describe will make much headway with voters because Americans are basically satisfied with a country that is peaceful, prosperous, and culturally tolerant. He finds much more cultural diversity, and thus political diversity, in America today than, say, 30 years ago, but he argues that people have managed to create a "political equilibrium" that may last for some time.

Terry Nichols Clark of the University of Chicago had discovered a similar mapping of political types in his studies of urban politics. Some mayors, he found, fall into categories other than what he calls the "traditional Republican" and the "traditional Democrat." These are the "ethnic politicians," who are as fiscally liberal as traditional Democrats but are less likely to be socially liberal; and the "new fiscal populists," who are fiscally conservative but socially liberal. (Confusingly enough, the people Clark calls new fiscal populists are similar to Maddox and Lilie's libertarians.) Clark found the new fiscal populists emerging in cities as diverse as Pittsburgh, Houston, New York, and San Francisco.

In the final chapter, journalist Paul Weaver reminds us that the larger changes in society frequently occur not in response to political leadership, but in spite of it. He argues that America's free-enterprise past is a myth, that for a century or more America has been a corporatist/managerialist society; since World War II, however, "this corporatist regime has weakened continually in every sphere—institutional, ideological, intellectual, cultural." Because of such new factors as the vigorous market for corporate control, the global economy, deregulation, the questioning attitude of young people, and the decline in respect for institutions, we are slowly moving toward a more individualist society, or, as Weaver puts it, "a kind of 'proto-neolibertarianism.' "

Edward H. Crane of the Cato Institute argues that the freedoms Americans enjoy today stem primarily from the active interest average Americans during the revolutionary period took in political ideas. At that time hundreds of thousands of Americans—in a population of 3 million—read and debated political ideas. What has changed? Crane argues that the rise of experts and the public school monopoly have discouraged widespread intellectual curiosity. Federal election laws have hampered new political movements, and the media have encouraged interest in politics as a horse race rather than as a contest of ideas. Crane urges opening up the system in a variety of ways—with tax credits to bring diversity to education, by abolishing the Federal Election Commission to bring more competition to politics, and by limiting the terms of members of Congress to eliminate the "permanent government" attitude in Washington.

Finally, historian Paul Kleppner of Northern Illinois University discusses how political leaders have used ideas to appeal to their supporters. He points to two major characteristics of contemporary politics. The first is the rise of the Religious Right, a movement with much precedent in American politics. Kleppner argues that while the Religious Right will win some electoral and legislative victories, "its success is likely to be fleeting because the movement swims against the tide of social and attitudinal change, tilts at the wrong windmills, and offers an inappropriate solution—public coercion rather than private conversion." The other major trend, he argues, is toward political specialization, the tendency for people to pick and choose among areas of political concern, which he sees as "a wholly rational response to a world . . . where the costs of acquiring information are high." If political leaders cannot meet the challenge of appealing both to specialists and to the broad grass roots of society, we will face a period of shifting coalitions and abrupt changes in policy.

The analysts in this book disagree on many issues, but they have identified the key problems that will determine the future course of American politics. One thing is clear: there are major social and political changes occurring in America, and political leaders will have to respond to them.

I. Trends in American Politics

William Schneider: The Democrats, I'm able to reveal, are in retreat. And I mean that literally. Last weekend, the Senate Democrats retreated to Shepherdstown, West Virginia, to discuss the future of their party. A few weeks ago, Democratic members of the House of Representatives went to White Sulphur Springs, West Virginia, on a retreat to think about the future of their party. There, under the salubrious influence of the West Virginia countryside, they heard an array of motivational experts ranging from Chrysler chairman Lee Iacocca to sports consultant Lou Tice and marketing strategist Ira Weinstein advise them on how to be winners. It's "in" to be in and it's "out" to be out, they were told, among many other things. Democratic intellectuals have been no less active—they're keeping up a frantic pace of seminars, forums, colloquiums, and symposia, all on more or less the same topic: whither the Democratic party?

In the past month I've participated in discussions sponsored by revisionist Social Democrats, French businessmen, Soviet academics, Republicans, Egyptian parliamentarians, and Democratic policy intellectuals at—where else?—Harvard. I did turn down an invitation, however, from the PLO. Democrats are desperate for ideas. At the beginning of February, in what was called his "coming-out" speech for 1988, Sen. Gary Hart called, unsurprisingly, for new ideas. He said, "Our past achievements are not a cathedral in which to worship but a firm foundation upon which to build a new vision. The party of change must change." That theme was echoed in March, surprisingly, by Sen. Edward Kennedy. "We have to realign our position," he said at Hofstra College. "Those of us who care about domestic progress must learn to do more with less."

I think we're well aware of how important ideas are in politics. The progressive movement had its intellectuals, like Herbert Croly, and its magazines, like the *Nation;* the New Deal had braintrusters; and John F. Kennedy's Camelot had the "best and the brightest." We're also well aware that most of the interesting new ideas in American politics during the past 10 years have come from the

11

right—from neoconservative intellectuals and supply siders and from magazines like the *Public Interest* and *Commentary*. Where are the intellectuals of the left? Where are the Democratic thinkers? Well, there are some self-styled neoliberals who are giving speeches in the Senate and writing articles in the *Washington Monthly*. But theirs, I think, is a fairly bloodless liberalism, more concerned with problem solving than with articulating a moral vision of society. We need something to compete with Reaganism, but it's going to have to be more compelling than high-tech investment credits and improved military-procurement policies.

Where are our magazines? The *New Republic* troubles many liberals, although it's the most influential journal among political intellectuals, because it seems to be drifting away from the left. The *New York Review of Books* has become a forum for exotic literary debate, and the *Village Voice* is mired in punk politics. Otherwise, what we read about is mostly consumerism and self-improvement. Of course, no one expects the Democrats to come back to power through the force of ideas. But ideas are crucial when the political moment comes. Here I'd like to bring up the example of the neoconservatives.

Many neoconservatives started out in the 1930s as left-wing Trotskyites. They became disillusioned with the Soviet Union, however, after the Moscow show trials and the Hitler-Stalin pact. They then discovered a great truth: that the Soviet Union is a brutal, corrupt, expansionist power, or, in the words of Susan Sontag, "a fascism of the left."

As Irving Kristol wrote, "The political moment for this point of view came in the 1950s. The Cold War gave these intellectuals influence and credibility. They had discovered the truth before anybody else." In the 1960s and 1970s, neoconservative intellectuals discovered another great truth: that many liberal social programs were not working. Indeed, these programs were making things worse on account of "unintended consequences"—the favorite phrase in the neoconservative dictionary. The welfare program was giving fathers an incentive to desert their families. The minimum wage was pricing many young people and poorly skilled workers out of the labor market. Urban renewal was displacing the poor. Rent control was depleting the supply of low-cost rental housing.

These penetrating criticisms were confined largely to intellectual journals until the political moment came. And that was in the late 1970s, when the great inflation in this country gave rise to a revolt

12

against government. It started in 1978 with Proposition 13 and the tax revolt and culminated in 1980 with the election of Ronald Reagan and the Republican takeover of the Senate. Suddenly the neoconservative critique, that government doesn't work the way it's supposed to work, became the prevailing public philosophy. Intellectuals once again had discovered a great truth whose time had come.

Let me argue here that we're beginning to discover another great truth in American politics. Many Democrats are beginning to see it, and we saw some evidence of it in the Hart and Kennedy speeches. We're discovering it as a result of our own experiences—particularly the Democratic party's experiences—both good ones and bad ones. The great truth is this: that all successful political innovation in this country is propelled by anti-establishment feeling. We Americans instinctively distrust concentrations of power, whether in government, business, labor, the press, or anywhere else. For instance, watch television sometimes to see how much sympathy there is for big shots, whether businessmen, politicians, or hospital administrators. Viewers, like voters (in fact, they *are* voters), enjoy seeing powerful people get what's coming to them.

Anti-establishment populism is neither liberal nor conservative, and politicians on both sides have used it effectively. It has been the most important force in politics for the past 20 years. For example, the last two presidents—one a Democrat, the other a Republican—both ran as anti-Washington candidates, outsiders who had little experience in national government. That was part of their appeal, just as it was for Andrew Jackson 150 years ago. The power of anti-establishment feeling was discovered independently by two political strategists, one from the right, the other from the left. The first to see it was Kevin Phillips, who, in *The Emerging Republican Majority* published in 1969, described the appeal of the New Right as based more on anti-establishment resentment than on ideology. At that time conservatives like Barry Goldwater and Ronald Reagan were concerned primarily with overthrowing the liberal Eastern establishment of the Republican party. But Phillips saw that the same energy could be used to challenge what they regarded as the liberal establishment that controlled the federal government.

In 1972, pollster Patrick Caddell masterminded George McGovern's seizure of the Democratic party. He saw what few others saw, namely, that a good part of McGovern's support was based not on ideology but on the fact that he was opposing the entrenched power of the Democratic party's regulars, men like Lyndon Johnson and

13

Hubert Humphrey, who thrived on the party's tradition of bosses and deals. That year Caddell promoted a theory of the alienated voter that argued that supporters of McGovern and supporters of George Wallace both opposed the Democratic party establishment. If the proper populist theme could be found—he suggested tax reform—then perhaps the two groups could form a potent anti-establishment coalition. It did not happen in 1972 because the ideological issues that separated the McGovern and Wallace voters—race and Vietnam—were stronger than the anti-establishment sentiment they shared. But to his credit, I think, Caddell stuck with his theory, and he made it work for Jimmy Carter in 1976.

Carter was exactly what the theory required: an outsider and a populist who had no clear ideological identification. He attracted just enough Wallace Democrats and just enough McGovern Democrats to squeak through the election. His opponent, President Ford, had already, of course, been softened up by an anti-establishment challenge in his own party from Ronald Reagan. Thus, the new-politics left in the Democratic party discovered the same thing that the New Right had discovered in the Republican party: that they had a "secret weapon" and that this weapon was anti-establishment feeling. It made them both seem vigorous and muscular and populist.

It showed up again last year in Hart's nearly successful challenge to Walter Mondale in the Democratic primaries. Mondale made the mistake of running as an insider—the candidate of the Democratic party establishment—in order to distance himself from Jimmy Carter. That made him vulnerable, just like his mentor Hubert Humphrey before him, to a challenge from yet another unknown, new-politics Democrat who was advised by Caddell.

There are many people in Washington who now believe that after Carter and Reagan, the anti-Washington issue has run its course. Mondale believed that, but it's not likely to be any more true in 1988 than it was in 1984. George Bush, who seems to be doing his best to imitate Mondale's campaign of inevitability, may end up learning the same lesson, namely, that anti-establishment feeling in the American electorate is very nearly inexhaustible.

The Democrats got caught on the wrong side of this issue. The party became identified with the status quo and the vested interests who had been running things in Washington for 50 years. To most Americans, the federal government had become the establishment. Defending it meant defending statism and interest-group liberal-

14

ism. Democrats tend to forget that the progressives and the New Deal liberals used government power to attack the vested interests and challenge the status quo. It sounds strange, but in those days government really was an anti-establishment force.

Now, as a result of Mondale's spectacular failure, Democrats are beginning to see the light. What they see so far is the need to curb the influence of organized so-called special interests inside the party. The newly elected chairman, Paul Kirk, began his tenure in office by refusing to support the Black Caucus's officially designated candidate for vice-chairman of the party and by advising organized labor not to endorse a presidential candidate before the 1988 primaries. Hart advised Democrats that "demands of the special-interest groups, including the party's own constituencies, should be important but secondary." Ted Kennedy, who went even further, said, "As Democrats we must understand that there's a difference between being a party that cares about labor and being a labor party. There's a difference between being a party that cares about women and being the women's party, and we can and must be a party that cares about minorities without being a minority party. We are citizens first and constituencies second."

All of this is good advice, but the special-interest issue is just a symbol of the larger problem: the identification of the Democrats with the government and the identification of government with the establishment and the status quo. Democratic strategists have to come up with ideas to change that perception, to make the power of government once again seem populist rather than elitist. Tax reform might be a good possibility but the problem is, the Republicans got to that issue first. It seems to me that the Democrats' problem is not to convince Americans that they want more government but to convince them, as Andrew Jackson and Theodore Roosevelt and Franklin Roosevelt did, that government is on their side.

Mervin Field: Bill Schneider's masterful talk painted a broad picture of some significant trends in American politics. What I'm going to do now is take Bill's binoculars and turn them around to focus on one set of trends in just one state, California. I'm going to describe an exercise that I think will be of interest as a demonstration of what happens when we look at the political spectrum in other than a conventional way.

We've been operating the California Poll now for almost 39 years.

15

We are in the field regularly, and we publish, in addition to the poll, a monthly report on opinion trends on a variety of subjects in California.

In one of our California opinion-index reports, we reported on the shift between 1970 and 1980 in the distribution of the public according to the traditional liberal-conservative scale. Let me describe the political context in California. California voters for some time have been very, very religious, first by law and ostensibly by inclination, in choosing between the two parties. Almost 9 out of 10 voters for the last 50 years have registered either as Democrats or as Republicans. Right now registration is about 53 percent Democratic and 36 percent Republican. The other 11 percent is composed of people who either "decline to state" or identified with minor parties. We're able to use this fairly rigid parameter as a validation of our samples. We also obtain information on how people classify themselves on the traditional liberal-conservative spectrum.

We ask, Do you consider yourself "conservative," "liberal," or "middle-of-the-road," or don't you think of yourself in these terms? If they say conservative or liberal, we then ask, Do you consider yourself a strong or a not-very-strong conservative or liberal? If they say middle-of-the-road, we ask, Do you think of yourself as being

Table 1

HOW CALIFORNIANS DESCRIBE THEMSELVES ON THE CONVENTIONAL IDEOLOGICAL SCALE, 1970 AND 1980 (%)

	Conservative	Middle-of-the-road	Liberal	No Opinion
Democrats				
1980	37	10	49	4
1970	32	27	32	9
Republicans				
1980	77	7	13	3
1970	61	19	14	6
Others				
1980	39	18	31	12
1970	29	22	28	21
Total				
1980	52	10	34	4
1970	42	23	26	9

Table 2

WHAT DO YOU MEAN WHEN YOU SAY YOU ARE CONSERVATIVE IN POLITICS?

Against large government/limit government	19%
For gradual (not radical) change	13
Government should eliminate waste/lower taxes	12
Against welfare/government giveaways	9
For self-initiative/self-determination	7
Believe in doing things the old way/status quo	7
Conserving on money/energy	6
Against liberal positions (general)	5
Believe in stronger defense/military posture	5
For free enterprise/capitalism	4
Being practical/getting results	3
Against judges who let criminals go free	3
Back the U.S./pro U.S.	2
Am conservative on fiscal issues (general)	2
Other mentions	18
Don't know/no answer	15

Table 3

WHAT DO YOU MEAN WHEN YOU SAY YOU ARE LIBERAL IN POLITICS?

Willing to change/new ideas	29%
For minority rights/individual rights	16
Gov't should help people/provide opportunities	13
Like liberal policies (general)	9
Not a conservative/against the right wing	5
For the environment	4
For the division of economic wealth	3
Against the draft/military spending increases	3
Because I am a Democrat	2
Other mentions	22
Don't know/no answer	15

Table 4

BRIEF DESCRIPTION OF FOUR IDEOLOGICAL CATEGORIES

Liberalism

Willing to regulate the economy. Support more government services and regulations. Favor government intervention to promote individual welfare. Outside economic realm, individual should be free of government restriction.

Populism

Support government regulation of the economy to prevent concentrations of wealth and to benefit "average man" or "little guy." Want more equal distribution of private property. Willing to use government to reestablish traditional American values. Support government power to regulate individual behavior so it conforms to traditional moral and social values.

Libertarianism

Emphasize autonomy of individual and minimal role of government. Want maximum individual choice in both economic and noneconomic realms. Can be achieved only if individual is free from government regulation. Advocate government nonintervention in both economic and personal-freedom area.

Conservatism

In economic realm oppose the use of government to restrict human behavior. Believe economic inequality is the natural consequence of inequalities in human ability and energy. See a need to use government authority and power to guide and limit human behavior in the realm of individual morals. Limits on personal behavior necessary to preserve society.

closer to conservative or closer to liberal? If they don't think of themselves in these terms at all, we then ask, If you had to choose, would you consider yourself conservative, liberal, or middle-of-the-road? Putting together the results of our surveys over the past 10 years, we find a big boost in the proportion of people identifying themselves as conservatives or liberals and a decline in the proportion classifying themselves as middle-of-the-road. (See Table 1.) We then asked the self-identified conservatives and liberals to tell us why they classified themselves that way, and you see the results in Tables 2 and 3.

We then asked our samples to tell us their positions on eight specific political and social issues. These were issues on which we could, I thought, produce a liberal-conservative dichotomy. The first statement was, "The government should see to it that every person is assured a job and a good wage." The conservative would disagree, and the liberal would agree.

Second, "Government health-care programs like Medicare should be expanded to cover all people in the population, regardless of age." The conservative would disagree, and the liberal would agree.

Third, "To make up for past discrimination, women and members of minority groups should be given special treatment in getting jobs and places in college." The conservative would disagree; the liberal would agree.

Fourth, "Business should be required to hire a certain number of minority workers and women, even if this means some whites and men would not be hired." The conservative would disagree, and the liberal would agree.

Fifth, "The military draft for men should be resumed." The liberal would disagree, and the conservative would agree.

Sixth, "Some people feel that we must do everything possible to protect the legal rights of those accused of committing crimes; others feel it is important to stop criminal activities even at the risk of reducing the rights of the accused. Which of these positions is closer to how you feel?" The conservative response would be that it's important to stop criminal activities, even at the risk of reducing the rights of the accused. The liberal would disagree.

Seventh, "If you had to choose, would you prefer a smaller government that provides fewer services, or would you prefer to have more services even if it means a larger government?" The conservative would prefer a smaller government; the liberal would disagree.

Last, "Do you think there should be more government regulation of business, less regulation, or about the same as there is now?" The conservative would prefer less regulation; the liberal, more or about the same.

In addition to the analysis I just showed you, the replies of the respondents in this survey were subjected to a classification analysis program that assigned respondents to groups based on the principle of maximizing differences between groups and minimizing differences within groups. What this means is that those individuals whose response patterns on the eight items were the most similar

Table 5

DEGREE OF AGREEMENT/SUPPORT FOR EIGHT POLITICAL/SOCIAL ISSUES BY FOUR IDEOLOGICAL GROUPINGS (%)

Issue	Liberal	Populist	Libertarian	Conservative
Government guarantee a job and good wage	89	99	17	1
Expand government health care programs	89	57	7	—
Special treatment of women/minorities in jobs/college placement	86	5	42	2
Require business hiring of women/minorities to make up for past discrimination	74	6	86	—
Resume military draft for men	49	56	53	64
Stop criminal activity at risk of reducing rights	43	57	41	61
Favor smaller government, providing fewer services	26	46	70	87
Favor less government regulation of business	18	29	50	72

Table 6

CALIFORNIA PUBLIC GROUPED ON REVISED POLITICAL SPECTRUM (%)

Liberal	21
Populist	19
Libertarian	14
Conservative	30
Divided/unclassifiable	16

to each other were grouped together. In this way we found four fairly distinct groups that conformed fairly well to the designations "liberal," "populist," "libertarian," and "conservative" (as defined in Table 4). This is a much different and perhaps more revealing distribution than the conventional liberal–middle-of-the-road–conservative typology.

Table 5 presents the distribution of respondents vis-à-vis the eight issues according to these four ideological groupings. Table 6 shows how the California public would divide on the revised political spectrum: liberals, 41 percent; populists, 19 percent; libertarians, 14 percent; conservatives, 30 percent; unclassifiable, 16 percent. Remember that the original chart showed liberals at 34 percent, conservatives at 52 percent, and the middle-of-the-road/no-opinion voters at 14 percent.

Dotty Lynch, moderator: I'd like to make a couple of comments—first, about the state of the Democratic party. Bill Schneider did not mention the words "masochism" and "self-flagellation," but I think they are very much a part of the Democrats' retreat mode.

Walter Mondale, who was the candidate of the establishment inside the Democratic party, allowed himself to be portrayed as the establishment candidate both by Gary Hart and Jesse Jackson and then by Ronald Reagan. One of the reasons for his massive defeat was exactly that, and yet inside the Democratic party you hear virtually no indictment of his candidacy on that point. After the 1972 election there was no such effort to spare the feelings of George McGovern, the anti-establishment candidate. The analysis of that election was that McGovern was the worst candidate the Democratic party could ever have put up because of his "amnesty, abortion," change-related attitudes.

Today no one criticizes Mondale for the opposite error, and I think in part it's because the Democratic establishment obviously would be indicting itself. Our difficulty in the Hart campaign in the summer of 1984 in trying to get the congressional delegates to the convention to support Senator Hart was astonishing to us. For the most part they admitted that Hart would probably be a stronger candidate but argued that he was somewhat unpredictable; at least with Mondale they knew what they were getting. They felt safe with Mondale; they didn't want to rock the boat. The top of the ticket would probably lose anyway, and they didn't want to risk something that they didn't quite understand.

One of the mistakes that Senator Kennedy may have made in his recent speech was getting involved in the ideological fight in the Democratic party. The concept of change—anti-establishment, if you will—that Senator Hart has had with him for his entire political career, both as campaign manager for George McGovern and as a candidate himself (which, incidentally, I think may be the cause of his being attracted to advisers like Pat Caddell and myself rather than the other way around), has been a deliberate attempt to be nonideological and may be a more successful political strategy than Kennedy's. Kennedy is obviously trying to get out of that very liberal mold that has hurt him. But by getting the litmus-test liberals angry with him, he may have missed the point of the power of the anti-establishment argument.

I'd like to return now for a moment to Mervin Field's presentation. I would be interested in seeing the figures for women voters and how they fit into the spectrum that Merv mentioned. What we see, in general, is that women have more of a belief that government has a role to play in social welfare issues. What has been curious to many is that the gender gap didn't work for the Democrats—women did not vote for Mondale even though Ferraro was on the ticket. Part of the reason was clearly a preemptive strategy on the part of the Republicans.

Richard Wirthlin, President Reagan's pollster, recently talked about a study of 45,000 women around the country. The women were placed in 1 of 64 different categories, based on various demographic characteristics. They were then grouped into about 8 categories, which were named "Alice," "Betty," "Carolyn," and on down to "Helen." The "Alice" category, composed of the younger professional women who were very excited about having a woman on the ticket, were as excited, or even more so, about their own personal lives. Reagan's people pitched a very strong part of their campaign on the economic-opportunity argument. They targeted women who were essentially independent—not those tied ideologically to one party or one philosophy—but those who were interested in their own futures and the futures of other women.

What we saw throughout the first Reagan administration were three components to the anti-Reagan feeling among women who opposed him: war and peace, the economy, and women's rights. The Mondale/Ferraro ticket essentially carried those women who felt that the war-and-peace issue and women's rights were very important and who gave Reagan little credit on either. The ticket lost many women who felt most strongly about the economic issue.

Women, because of their other-directedness, their increasing likelihood to be in the workplace their entire lives, and their tendency to be very specific and practical in their relationship to the political system, are willing to support more government intervention than male voters. I think the political strategy that takes this fact into account is the one that will be successful.

Question: *Almost all anti-establishment feelings stem from a desire for change. The depression brought forth the major changes in government of the 1930s, and the movement to the right in the 1970s was a reaction to stagflation—high inflation and high unemployment. There may again be a period of anti-establishment feeling or desire for change because of global trade circumstances. It would not surprise me to see a new party in the future—an anti–free-trade party. What is your feeling about this?*

Field: Those are far-ranging assertions. I would predict a very dismal outlook for any new party. There can be new ideas within the existing parties—new ideas transcending established or antiquated ideas—and perhaps new movements within the existing parties. But the whole weight of our system is such that it makes it difficult, if not impossible, for any new party to gain ascendancy.

Schneider: While people think that free trade is a nice idea, they strongly support tariff barriers and import quotas. It is a populist issue, not a liberal or conservative issue. In the late 1970s, when we had the great inflation, pollsters explained to people that free trade would benefit consumers because it would hold down prices of both domestic and imported goods. On the other hand, to be fair, the argument was presented that free trade hurts American business and endangers American jobs. When asked to choose a position, the public didn't budge. They were still about three-to-one in favor of tariff barriers and import quotas.

This leads me to conclude that when people answer questions like that, they are not calculating their own interests as consumers. What they are doing is giving what they perceive is the right answer. The right moral answer is, "I should not benefit as a consumer at the expense of American workers."

What has held protectionism back in this country is the fairly unified sentiment on the part of the elite that free trade is really the better way. Whenever a politician, whether John Connally in 1980 or Walter Mondale in 1983, makes a vaguely protectionist speech, the entire establishment jumps on him and accuses him of pandering to popular sentiment and prejudice. Critical editorials appear in the *Washington Post* and the *New York Times*, so the politician backs away. It's mostly anti-establishment politicians, like George Wallace and Jesse Jackson, who are able to make protectionist speeches outright because they don't care what the establishment says about them.

The big change we are seeing now is the elite beginning to back off from its commitment to free trade, at least in fact if not in principle. This is mostly because when American businessmen can't compete with foreign imports, they say it's *not* because U.S. industry is inefficient or poorly managed but because of a situation that is not their fault—namely, the overvaluation of the dollar. That is why we have a flood of imports and can't sell our goods abroad. My view is that if the establishment cracks on this issue—if businessmen and politicians abandon free trade, as we are beginning to see—the public will be very ready to follow their lead.

Question: *Mr. Schneider, if you are telling us that changes in American politics occur because of anti-establishment ideas that have a populist flavor, there seems to be a paradox in the current American electoral scene. We have a House of Representatives that should be more responsive to changes in the mass electorate. Yet we don't see the changes of recent years reflected in the House. I wonder if you might offer an explanation as to why no one talks seriously about the House having a Republican majority in the near future.*

Schneider: I can explain it with one word: incumbency. One of the other trends not often spoken about in American politics is that incumbency has come to be more and more important in lower-level offices. It has much to do with the media. If you don't get on television, you don't exist. For the most part, House challengers don't get on television. There is one irrefutable rule: people don't vote for someone they've never heard of. Polls show this year after year. Incumbents are well known and widely heard of; they use the power of their office—computerized letters, direct mail, etc.—to keep in contact with their constituents. Nobody has ever heard of the challengers.

Most people have heard of Senate challengers, however, which is why we have a reasonably high turnover in the Senate. Everyone has heard of presidential contenders; most people have heard of gubernatorial contenders because they are covered on television. One of the trends we are seeing in the House and lower level offices, and one of the reasons why the Republicans have not made further headway, is that the people who go to the voting booth are not particularly ideological or partisan. They see the name of a familiar and favorably regarded incumbent, and even if they don't agree with the incumbent's position—they probably don't even know what the position is—if they've never heard of the challenger, they vote for the incumbent. House members have become very adroit at making themselves favorably regarded by their constituents. For the most part, they do so by avoiding issues and by simply doing constituency service and keeping in touch. Challengers try unsuccessfully to challenge House members on the issues, but they have the enormous barrier of name recognition and familiarity to overcome.

Lynch: The actual vote for the House races in 1984, however, was closer than the number of seats gained would indicate. The irony is that the Republicans spent a tremendous amount of money in anticipation of the 1980 elections on legislative races to redraw the lines of districts so that they would not face the problems they have had in gerrymandering. But in some states, despite computers, large sums of money, and technology, Democratic state legislatures were able to keep the lines in fairly good order so that they maintained those seats.

Question: *As a follow-up to that point, political action committees in Washington tend to support the incumbent. Do you feel that the anti-*

establishment "populist" voting in the grass roots might be in conflict with the PACs' support of incumbents?

Field: PACs, because they now can aggregate and dispense money judiciously in respect to their interests, reaffirm the power of incumbency. At one level, issues and broad themes are not seen operating. We've all seen poll data in congressional races that show large proportions and majorities that do not know their congressperson. They have a difficult time citing even one position that the incumbent or challenger might have. It's almost as if they don't care. It is only when you have presidential or gubernatorial candidates taking certain issues and creating a tide, and that tide starts filtering down, that you gain the public's attention. For example, in the 1984 election, Democratic candidates for offices below the president, recognizing the outcome, left the sinking ship, and ran their own candidacies because the party structure was so weak. In California, parties are almost a joke.

If you are a successful candidate, you go to PACs, which are the money trees. Everyone complains about raising money, but each year there is a big increase in the total amount raised. The process is operating on a variety of tracks; issues and broad themes take a lot of time and must generate a lot of force before they affect outcomes of races at the lower levels.

Schneider: I think we've hit on a two-sided theory here. The principal force of change is what I described as anti-establishment feeling—this interest in shaking things up—a populist resentment of insiders and people who control things in all institutions, not just government. Slowing that down is the major inertial force in our politics—the power of incumbency—which has become very great in recent years, particularly in lower-level offices. It has helped the Democrats immensely: they owe their survival to incumbency. If the government had passed a law in 1984 saying that no incumbent was eligible to run for reelection, the Republicans would have swept the elections.

As far as PACs are concerned, it has been discovered that if you give money to incumbents, it doesn't make much difference in terms of votes. Money spent on incumbents, whether in large or small sums, doesn't have much effect on the number of votes they get. But money spent on challengers means a great deal—money buys name recognition. A well-financed challenger can buy the media time to get the name recognition critical to being taken as a serious candidate. Without any money, the candidate doesn't exist. There is an imbalance, and PACs are beginning to discover it.

Question: *Last fall, pollster Vic Fingerhut conducted a poll in nine industrial states and suggested that in order for Mondale to win the election, he needed to attract people whom Fingerhut identified as the "weak Democrats." He stated that the way to bring those people back into the Democratic party, at least at the presidential level, was to turn to traditional Democratic themes and talk about Kennedy, Truman, and Roosevelt. The president also recognized this, for he made many references throughout the campaign to those people. He talked about how he didn't leave the Democratic party but the Democratic party left him. I am wondering how that analysis fits in with what you are talking about.*

Lynch: One of the difficulties with that strategy, and one that we saw consistently in the data, was that the "weak Democrats" were more hostile to Mondale than were independent voters. Independent voters had problems with both candidates but tended to be somewhat more "getable" than the "weak Democrats." The second problem with the strategy was that Mondale was already suffering from a very heavy association with the past. By continuing to exploit that association, he would have further turned off those independent and potentially persuadable voters who tended to be ticket-splitters or suburban Republican/Gary Hart–type of voters. Those "weak Democrats" had voted Democratic in the past, but Reagan did a very good job of convincing them that he was the true heir to that legacy.

Schneider: The "weak Democrats" include two streams of Democrats that have been leaving the party in enormous numbers in the past 20 years—white southerners, who are traditional Democrats but not liberal, and urban, working-class ethnic voters outside the South—the "Archie Bunker" vote. The Democratic party has moved to the left; the Republican party has moved to the right. These people don't feel comfortable in either party. Great numbers left the Democratic party in 1968 with Humphrey, in 1972 with McGovern, and again in 1984 with Mondale. Many came back with Carter in 1976.

Remember what the Republicans kept excoriating in Dallas—the "San Francisco Democrats." They said that the Democrats were too liberal for their traditional constituents—those Democrats who

27

couldn't go along with the direction the party had taken in 1968, when it moved to the left on race. So white Southern racists left the party and have not come back. Those who left in 1972 with McGovern were mostly neoconservatives who didn't like the direction the party took on foreign policy. The party's shift to the left in 1968 and 1972 is irreversible, and conservative Democrats are not going to come back in very large numbers. If they are truly conservative, they are just not going to be comfortable in the Democratic party. That's a big loss. Ronald Reagan, John Connally, Strom Thurmond, and Jesse Helms all used to be Democrats. But they were conservatives who didn't feel at home in the party. They left, taking most of their supporters with them, and they're not coming back.

The real issue is this—not what happened in 1968 and 1972, but what happened in 1980 and 1984, which I hope *is* reversible. (I'm speaking as a Democrat.) What happened in 1980 and 1984 had nothing to do with race or foreign policy. It had to do with the economy. The Democrats lost economic credibility. It is the economic issue that has held the Democratic party together for 50 years as the party that would protect ordinary working people against adversity. That is economic populism. The party can still pull itself together if it can regain its economic populism and credibility.

Thomas Moore, *Fortune*: *When you speak of populist and anti-establishment feeling, to what extent is that feeling economically motivated or instead motivated by concerns about social policy issues?*

Schneider: My feeling is that the Democrats historically have had an economic populist appeal and that the Republicans have developed in recent years a social populist appeal: traditional moral values, and resistance to cultural change and the more exotic forms of social liberalism. What I am suggesting is a funny sort of mixture. The Democrats, in a nutshell, have become economically populist and socially elitist. The Republicans have become socially populist and economically elitist, the party of the rich. Now the Democrats risk losing their economic populism, which is devastating. If the Democrats have no economic populism, they have no populism at all.

What Jack Kemp and the Conservative Opportunity Society Republicans are saying is that maybe the Republican party—on top of its social populism, which Reagan very much has—can acquire a kind of economic populism and lose its image as the party of the rich, the party of interests, and the party of big business. That is why Reagan makes overtures to labor-union members and talks about the conservative opportunity society, using vigorous, muscular, populist terms to steal the thunder from the Democrats. I don't think the Republicans have really acquired that sort of economic populism yet, but the Democrats are in serious danger of losing theirs. Without that economically populist appeal, the Democratic party becomes nothing but a liberal party, a party of educated, upper middle-class liberals and minorities. That is not a winning coalition.

David Boaz, Cato Institute: *Mr. Field, do you think the evidence you presented here today should make a difference to a candidate or a campaign manager planning a campaign in California? If so, what would be the considerations for a Republican or a Democrat?*

Field: I'm not a candidate, but I am a believer in the idea that information is power. I'm not so sure parties or candidates subscribe to that view. The problem in considering the trends I described in my paper and relating them to ground-level politics in California requires a very big stretch. California supported Ronald Reagan by a large margin very similar to the national popular margin. It has voted Republican in all presidential elections since 1964. A candidate must recognize that straight partisan appeals or conventional ideological appeals just won't work. When you talk about someone being conservative on an economic issue and liberal on a social or cultural issue, or vice versa, people understand that. But the terms "populism" and "libertarianism" are not readily understandable. If a candidate could reduce these terms to their elements and portray the ideological conflict within every voter, he might be able to appeal to more voters.

II. The Politics of the Baby Boom

Lee Atwater: The baby-boom phenomenon has become somewhat caricatured as the "yuppie" movement, but it's important to understand that this so-called pig in the python, the baby boom, is probably going to be the single most important political phenomenon for the next 15 or 20 years. This group has dominated American culture in one form or another since it came into being.

If you take the point of view that the baby boomers are those born between 1946 and 1964, you see that all the way back in 1953 or 1954 the marketing community understood the importance of this group. The very first mass-market fad in this country was the Davy Crockett boomlet, which I remember very well. The fad started in late September or October, when literally every kid in America was getting Davy Crockett stuff. But by mid-November the thing fell flat; the kids were moving on to something else. Three or four or years later some people figured out that the baby-boom group had grown a little older and that parents were willing to spend about 50 percent on the male and 50 percent on the female. So they came up with a new fad for the baby-boom—the hula hoop—and, sure enough, for about two weeks you could not walk out of the house without seeing everybody else with hula hoops. When this same group was three or four years older, someone thought, well, let's knock away the plastic and put a little extra sex in it, and so the "twist" came along.

A couple of years after that came the Beatles. And for the next four or five years the Beatles went right along with this group as it moved into the psychedelic head music of the sixties. At that time, of course, the Vietnam war was a very important cultural experience in America, and the baby boom was right in the center of it, as it was with the entire "movement of the sixties."

The next development in American culture was the disco movement. By this time, the baby boomers were in their mid-twenties, and you had what Christopher Lasch has termed the "culture of narcissism" that came to fruition in the mid- to late seventies. I'm

31

sure Pat remembers this whole period well, which was symbolized by the "malaise" speech of President Carter.

Then the group moved into mental awareness and self-improvement. As they got a little wider in the waist and a little slower in the head, jogging became popular, which takes us up to today, when I believe economic and political activity is coming to be at the forefront of baby-boom activities.

So the baby boomers are coming into political awareness at the same time that demographics dictate that by 1988 they will represent about 60 percent of the electorate—and that is real political and economic power.

Now, what does all this mean? Why is this group different? Let me provide some historical perspective. In order to understand this generation, you have to look at the generation that came before it, which basically had two major political experiences: the depression and World War II. Those 20 years led to almost a survivalist mentality. You didn't have leisure time—basically, you were worrying from one day to the next where your meals were going to come from. These values are extremely different from the lifestyle and values developed by the baby boomers.

Also during this period, Franklin Roosevelt re-invented the American government—the whole concept of government and how it worked. The federal government was seen as playing an almost heroic role in American life during that time. In a word, the values that this group grew up with were materialistic.

Now, they went out to fight World War II. They came back and had a lot of kids. That's the baby boom. How did they grow up? Or how did we grow up, speaking as a fellow baby boomer? We grew up in the fifties, sixties, and seventies. In the fifties, first of all, you had one of the most important revolutions in the history of any society—the television revolution. Suddenly a group went from nothing of this kind to five-and-a-half hours of uncontrolled information coming into their homes a day.

Second, because of the experience our parents had, they got out and through thrift, hard work, and materialistic values they provided a middle-class lifestyle enabling baby-boom kids to grow up with unprecedented educational opportunities. And education looms very large in understanding the difference between the baby boom and other generations.

Also occurring in the fifties was the beginning of the most important demographic change in America in the last 30 years—the integration of women into the workforce. In the year I was born, some 30 percent of women were in the workforce. Now, of course, about 52 percent are working. So I would say education is the number-one difference in this generation; the number-two difference is the role of women in society.

Leisure time was something else this group had in abundance in the fifties and sixties. In the sixties, of course, you had an even greater new value scale, which was the whole Vietnam experience. In the colleges at that time were millions of kids with unprecedented leisure time—time to think. History shows that when certain materialistic goals are achieved, people move into a new state of consciousness. This is, in effect, what began to happen in the sixties. Vietnam had an unbelievable effect on the value structure of these people.

The Kennedy assassination, I think, is somewhat overemphasized, but I do think that it was the first world community event, and the baby boomers, again, were right in the middle of it. You can't find anyone in this group who can't tell you what class he was in, who the teacher was, and exactly where he was the instant he heard that John Kennedy was shot. I don't think the event itself was as important as the concept of the first world community media event.

So, in the seventies you had Watergate, inflation, the oil crisis, and, of course, the "malaise" speech, which did reflect the concept of a national malaise throughout the country. The blending of the values of these three decades—the materialism of the fifties and the new consciousness of the sixties culminating in the seventies— led up to what I call the "new values" of today.

Now, I think that in order to examine these new values, you've got to think of them in conjunction with what else is going on, and that is a technology revolution. When you move from an industrial age into Alvin Toffler's Third Wave, or into the communication or information age, you've got two forces working simultaneously that are very important—a cultural value revolution and a technology revolution. They add up to what I call a "new synthesis," for lack of a better term.

What are the components of this new synthesis? One of them is the concept of "self-actualization," or "inner direction." Daniel Yankelovich's *New Rules* is illuminating in this area, and the VALS group at Stanford has come out with another useful book called *Nine American Lifestyles*, written by Arnold Mitchell. According to these books, once you get certain materialistic needs taken care of, you start looking for self-actualization and inner directedness. This inner-directed movement is characteristic of the baby-boom generation.

It manifests itself in several other issues too. One is the concept of quality. Bigger is not better anymore—better is better. That's one of the things that the Hart campaign understood very clearly. To the extent that the yuppie movement is caricatured, it is on the notion that excellence means Rolex watches, BMWs, fern bars, and so on. But if you read books such as *In Search of Excellence,* you will understand that there is a new drive for true excellence in this country that's very important.

The concept of opportunity is also a part of this new value synthesis. It involves equal opportunity and upward opportunity, and I think the role of minorities and women is an integral part of it. Baby boomers feel that all groups should have opportunity.

It's popular to say that baby boomers are economic conservatives but liberals on social issues, but I don't quite look at it that way. Rather than viewing them as "liberal" on social issues, the concept and the word should be "tolerance." In other words, there is almost a new traditionalism. They do understand the concept of family, and the family's very important to them, but they understand that the very structure of the family unit has changed. The concept of hard work is still intact, but it's not hard work for the sake of money or for materialism; it's hard work with a notion of success in mind, instead of just money. On the other hand, on issues such as sexual mores, smoking marijuana maybe, cohabitation, and so on, you find them liberal or at least open-minded.

Another component of this new value structure is social conscience. The social consciousness that developed in this group in the 1960s has stayed intact. That's why you see issues like South Africa emerging now, as well as the hunger issue and others. This keen social consciousness is a distinguishing trait of this group.

The role of women is seen by this group as coequal with men. The integration of women into the work force has helped create this, but baby boomers generally feel that equality is the name of the game. Issues like equal pay will be very high on their agenda.

Also very important to this group is the concept of "anti-big," and again I have to give credit to the Hart people for understanding that notion as they approached the New Hampshire campaign. Baby boomers are by and large anti–big government, anti–big labor unions, and anti–big institutions in general. What we as Republicans have always got to be aware of is that they're also anti–big business, and if we once again become viewed as the party that caters solely to big business, we would be in trouble with this group.

And then there's the notion of change. This group is not liberal, and I don't think they ever will be. But they are liberal in the sense that they understand the concept of change, and they will be by and large more receptive to change throughout their lives than any other group.

Last, there is a broad concept that I don't know how to articulate concisely. I've looked over a lot of interviews with baby boomers in the last few months, and even those who are supposedly happy— both economically and with their families—feel there's something missing in their lives. When you ask them the right questions you elicit this feeling, yet they can't seem to explain what it is. You find a gulf between their values and their lifestyle. Their lifestyle is somewhat different from their expressed values, and this gulf of cognitive dissonance, if you want to use the scholarly term for it, must be closed. Candidates who understand this gulf and try to make values and lifestyles work together for this group are going to do very well.

What are the issues in the future for this group? Tax reform, particularly the flat tax, is going to be right at the top of the agenda as these people get squeezed economically. Education will be a critical issue, and health care is very important. Baby boomers are already faced with the health-care problems of their parents and relatives, and very soon they are going to be faced with health problems of their own. Day care is no longer a liberal-conservative issue, but one that virtually all baby boomers are vitally interested in. Concern for the environment is now a consensus issue, no longer a liberal-conservative issue, among baby boomers. In regard to national defense, baby boomers do understand that there's a threat out there; they are conservative, but they want a more efficient national defense. Star Wars will be an exciting concept to them. They want better, more efficient weapons, but they want to spend less money.

Now what does all this amount to for the parties? In any party structure that has a winner-take-all provision, which our American government has, there are always going to be two parties. You'll have periods when a third party will emerge, which may actually engulf one of the other parties, but ultimately you always go back to a two-party structure because of the winner-take-all provision—and the Federal Election Commission has in any event created a situation in which it's going to be very hard for another party to come in.

I do think that we're off the flat liberal-conservative or Republican-Democratic continuum and into a four-pronged continuum composed of populists, libertarians, conservatives, and liberals. Each year the populists will probably diminish in number and the libertarians will grow larger and larger as a result of the influx of the baby boomers into the decision system.

David Boaz: Ever since the baby boom began in 1946, marketing experts have been anticipating the changes that such a huge generation would entail. Some 75 million Americans were born between 1946 and 1964, and as they grew up they influenced every area of American life: the baby-food industry, elementary schools, television, colleges, and the workplace. They have also, of course, had an impact on politics, beginning in the 1960s.

As a result of both the baby boom and the affluence of the 1950s, the largest generation in history began entering college in about 1964. The affluence and the expanded lifestyle choices that always accompany prosperity brought about an increased interest in personal freedom among the young, while provoking a reaction by other sectors of society against "permissiveness." This interest in freedom was greatly enhanced by the invention of the Pill, which swept away centuries of taboos and brought about a sexual revolution. And, of course, this huge college population collided with the most unpopular war in American experience, in what one observer has called "a hellish blind date arranged by history." Campus turbulence helped create the presidential candidacies of Robert Kennedy and Eugene McCarthy and may, ironically, have made Ronald Reagan governor and Richard Nixon president.

After Nixon's 1974 resignation brought "the Sixties" to a close, however, the baby boomers seemed to disappear as a political force. The political system became quieter, though hardly more successful. The first stirrings of the adult baby boom could be noted in 1980, when John Anderson did twice as well among voters under 35 as among older voters.

But it was in 1984 that the baby boom and especially the young urban professionals, or "yuppies," really came to the attention of political observers. The yuppies appeared to be the base of Gary

Hart's support in the Democratic primaries. Hart's success was not just generational: he seemed to have projected an image that was simultaneously to the right and left of Walter Mondale, as noted by frustrated journalists. But Hart was not picking his issues at random. He was to the left of Mondale on cultural and foreign-policy issues, while seeming to attack Mondale's New Deal economics from the right. He was breaking all the rules, but it seemed to be working. Mondale TV ads charged that "Gary Hart opposed the Chrysler rescue plan and the windfall profits tax," and yuppie viewers replied, "Sounds good to me."

Journalists began to examine this new group in the electorate. The *New York Times* pronounced them economically conservative, socially liberal, and voicing a "thunderous no" on military intervention. A Harris poll found baby boomers more in favor of defense spending cuts and deregulation and more opposed to protectionism and special help for smokestack industries than older voters. They were also more inclined to call themselves independents.

These economic and political perspectives are solidly rooted in the life experiences of the baby-boom generation. They—we—don't remember the Depression or World War II; a different set of political events formed our impressions. Consider a voter who will be 37 in 1988: He was 11 during the Cuban missile crisis, when his class-mates huddled in the hall during air-raid drills and learned of the imminent threat of nuclear war. He was 14 when the bombing of North Vietnam began, 18 and trying to avoid the draft when the number of U.S. troops in Vietnam peaked, 23 when President Nixon resigned in disgrace, and 29 when inflation hit double digits under President Carter.

Vietnam, Watergate, the cultural revolution of the sixties, and stagflation gave our generation a very different view of government from that of our parents. One question, of course, is whether these younger voters will, as conventional wisdom would have it, get more conservative as they get older. I think not. As baby boom author Landon Jones puts it, "The question to ask regarding a person's politics—or a generation's—is not how old the person is but when the person was young."

In any case, ultimately the yuppies weren't enough to win Hart a Democratic nomination, and younger voters found themselves faced with a choice between Walter Mondale and Ronald Reagan. They seemed to prefer Reagan's economic policies, but they were wary of his views on social issues and foreign policy. Reagan's advisers were aware of this. Pollster Richard Wirthlin found young voters "very individualistic in their economic views but quite liberal in terms of their positions on social issues, such as the ERA and abortion." Lee Atwater, then deputy director of the Reagan campaign, said Reagan must "maintain the fact, as he always has, that he is tolerant." Another Reagan adviser said that the baby boomers "are more susceptible to turning against us on foreign policy than the older Democrats."

Reagan successfully dispelled these fears for the most part. Despite constant conservative rhetoric on the social issues during his first term, he had managed not to win any of those battles and thus avoided a backlash among young voters. Also, he turned down an invitation on a nationally televised press conference to attack the Democrats for their support of gay rights, saying merely, "I just have to say I am opposed to discrimination period." After four years of "evil empire" rhetoric, he suddenly found the time to meet with Soviet foreign minister Andrei Gromyko just before the election and announced a planned resumption of arms talks.

Mondale failed to persuade the yuppies that a vote for Reagan really meant that they were joining Jerry Falwell's party, and Reagan did especially well among young voters on election day. Although he got only 4 percent of Mondale's primary voters and 6 percent of Jesse Jackson's, he gained the support of 34 percent of Hart's primary voters. Perhaps most significantly, 62 percent of self-described young urban professionals voted for Reagan.

As we look toward 1988, however, it appears that no presidential candidate has yet perfected his sales pitch to the yuppies. Despite all the evidence, observers still don't quite understand the baby-boom generation. Too many traditional analysts and politicians are still trying to figure out whether they're "really" liberals or conservatives. The problem is, those labels just don't work anymore.

As Maddox and Lilie pointed out in their book *Beyond Liberal and Conservative*, we have traditionally divided people into two political categories: liberals, who favor government intervention in the economy and oppose it in personal lives; and conservatives, who favor intervention in "moral" questions and oppose it in the economy. But Maddox and Lilie found that there are an equal number of Americans who logically belong in two new categories: populists, who favor government intervention in both areas; and libertarians, who oppose it in both areas.

There are, of course, strong demographic differences among these four groups. In particular, the libertarians tend to be younger, better educated, and more affluent—just the definition of a yuppie. Libertarians rose from 9 percent of the population in 1972 to 18 percent by 1980. And after accounting for voter turnout, the four groups are amazingly close: out of every 100 adult Americans in 1980, the 54 who went to the polls included 12 liberals, 11 conservatives, 12 libertarians, and 13 populists (and 6 not classifiable).

For a variety of reasons it seems likely that the libertarian group will continue to grow: the increasing educational level of the electorate, the continuing—though less explosive—spread of the cultural revolutions of the sixties throughout society, the expansion of high-tech and service industries at the expense of smokestack industries, and the increasing appreciation for the free market.

If that is true, then candidates of both parties ought to be focusing their efforts on how to attract the baby-boom or "libertarian" vote. This is a difficult problem, though, and there are powerful psychological and institutional obstacles to such new approaches within each party. Republican pollster Lance Tarrance points out the Democrats' problems with younger voters: "Unions, high wages, protectionism—all tied to the parts of the country that won't change. These people see the Democrats as locking the country in." On the other hand, another Republican pollster, Robert Teeter, acknowledges that "an increasing number of better-educated voters are tolerant of a wider range of lifestyles and may not react well to our position on some of these [social and moral] issues."

Despite the disaster of the Mondale campaign, labor is not likely to loosen its grip on the Democratic party. It seems likely that a yuppie-oriented candidate would have to fight tooth-and-nail to overcome union influence on the Democratic nominating process—though interviews with a number of Hart delegates to last year's convention would suggest that there is a Democratic constituency fed up with union power and ready to take the unions on. A Republican candidate, on the other hand, would have to win his party's nomination over the opposition of the Moral Majority and the socially conservative voters. Those voters may be declining in number, but their leaders are not ready to give up. Said one GOP organizer at the Dallas convention, "I think 1980 was the heyday of traditional values because the older conservatives are dying off. As they become fewer they become more strident in insisting they're the majority." Today, New Right leaders are pushing Rep. Jack

Kemp to reduce his emphasis on taxes and the economy and affirm has commitment to social conservatism, a sure turn-off for yuppies.

Entrepreneurs have arisen to satisfy every other desire of the baby boom, from hula hoops to Saabs. Political entrepreneurship, however, is more difficult for a number of reasons. Unlike the marketplace, the political consumer has to accept a package deal that he may not like; he can't try a little bit of a product and change his mind easily; and it is much more difficult to obtain reliable information in the political market.

For a candidate to appeal to the yuppie market, he or she would have to give up a "safe" coalition—the labor-liberal road to the Democratic nomination, or the orthodox conservative approach on the Republican side—in favor of trying something that offers a high potential for gain but great risks as well. Gary Hart, who seemed to have an early start on the yuppie constituency, is continuing his unfortunate commitment to industrial policy and recently made a major speech proposing universal national service as a "new idea." The beauty of national service as a political theme is that it would burden only those who currently can't vote, but it's hardly in sync with the yuppie outlook. On the Republican side of the aisle most of the potential candidates seem to be moving toward a more socially conservative approach, trying to combine a conservative base with populists rather than with libertarians.

If the Republicans were smart, they would combine their fiscally conservative constituency with the yuppies instead of the Moral Majority, creating a forward-looking rather than backward-looking coalition. If the Democrats were smart, they would move more forthrightly toward the market-oriented policies that Gary Hart only hinted at, combining them with their liberal views on cultural and foreign-policy issues, and thus try to add the yuppies to their traditional peace and civil-liberties constituencies.

One of my favorite writers, Michael Kinsley, wrote recently in the *New Republic* that the Democrats can appeal to young voters on personal-freedom issues. He pointed out that "the younger voters both parties are so desperate to attract have little interest in seeing greater government control over their lives. Even the post-1960s kids who went for Reagan in such astonishing numbers are far more likely than their elders to take a tolerant view of abortion, drug use, homosexuality, and so on." So Kinsley urges the Democrats to emphasize their support for personal freedom and wait for the voters to tire of Republican economic policies. But why shouldn't the Democrats instead combine their social tolerance with an economic program that is as good as or better than Republican economics? They could do worse than to adopt the *New Republic's* economics. (They could do better, but let's not hope for miracles.) Perhaps Kinsley thinks it's futile to urge the Democrats toward sound economics. But his approach condemns us to the same old choice: social tolerance and economic insanity from the Democrats, or reasonably sound economics and the Moral Majority from the Republicans. I think the Me Generation should demand something better.

Just as entrepreneurship doesn't follow established patterns but breaks them—giving us not just better products but new concepts, like personal computers, VCRs, and Federal Express—political entrepreneurship is likely to come from unexpected places. The politician who sees the yuppie market and capitalizes on it may be not an established name but someone we haven't yet heard of.

Imagine a candidate with the free-market views of, say, Jack Kemp and the cultural and foreign-policy liberalism of Gary Hart, and you have a campaign that could attract younger voters into either party and shape the political future for a generation. But such a candidate would face powerful resistance in either party. The future of American politics may be determined by whether the Democrats can liberate themselves from the grip of the AFL-CIO before the Republicans break free from the Moral Majority.

Pat Caddell: Some people believe that the classic sociological definition of baby boomers is those people born between 1946 and 1964. I tend to think sociologically it started sooner because it has to do less with chronology of years than with the period of experience. So I think you could take the baby boom back a few years to include people in their early forties, rather than cutting it off at age 39. In other words, those people born toward the middle to the end of World War II are really on the front edge of the baby-boom generation. And I think you can pretty well cut it off at age 25. In other words, those people born in 1960 or later have had different experiences, and their attitudes don't really fit in with those of the baby boomers, except in a limited way on some cultural issues.

But it doesn't really matter. No matter where you cut it, you are dealing with the single largest generation in the whole American experience. And therefore its potential in politics is great. As Lee pointed out, it potentially will make up 60 percent of the electorate in 1988. It has already had enormous political impact on the political process, as I'm going to point out, even though it still lags behind terribly in its voting participation. Even the older edge of the baby-boom generation does not match the voter turnout of other cohorts in past years as they've reached their late thirties and forties. In other words, the rush of participation of previous generations at the time they reached their thirties has still not been matched by the baby boom. But the baby boom is so big that even at lesser percentages the numbers are overwhelming in terms of impact. So when we talk about the potential impact, you have to understand not only what is there but what more there could be if someone could invigorate it or make it more activist in the political sector.

So the first thing that you have is size. And what size gives you is the position of critical mass. This is a generation different from other generations because it is essentially self-contained. It is so big and forceful that all through its existence it has experienced itself as the center of events. The baby boomers have not been tagging along; from the time they were born, they have been the center of attention. This experience breeds a certain arrogance.

In addition, its critical-mass size has allowed it the feeling, as I said, of being self-contained in that the communication is genera-tion-wide. Those of you who saw *The Big Chill* know that the movie depicts a generation in which pictures, remembrances, ideas, and experiences are shared universally, and music is the greatest con-ductor of these. That's what I mean when I talk about there being a networking of grass roots, a networking of experiences, of pictures and words and music, that in fact allowed communication across the whole generation. Its experiences—particularly the cultural and social ones—span a generation.

Many of the younger members of Congress in both parties have found that they have a lot more in common with each other than they expected. They understood each other; they could speak to each other. They came from the same frame of reference. They got along better together than they did with their older, ideological compatriots. The division was generational.

You can't understand politics without understanding social and cultural events. We are so Ptolemaic here in Washington; we think the world revolves around us. I look at the list of participants in this conference. We're all people who live inside the Beltway, we think what we do is important, we think what's going on here is important, and we think we're important people. The truth is, we're irrelevant to most people. The things that really drive society are not centered here in terms of politics; they're centered in cultural and social movements, which we don't spend enough time examining. And this is a generation that imposed its social and cultural changes on the entire country. It did that in the sixties with music—the end of Elvis Presley and the beginning of the Beatles, the revolution in music. It even influences the younger generation today. The baby boomers are the ones who forced the change in tolerance and in social attitudes about sex and other things in society, and they are the ones who essentially forced the ratification on the questions of race and women in society. They have imposed their view. So when Lee says it's a very unhappy generation in some ways, you have to go back and look at those experiences to understand its impact on society and the lack of any real focus about where it's going.

So the issue of critical mass is enormously important. Peter Drucker pointed out that when the baby boom hit college, the median age of the country dropped within a couple of years from about 38 or 39 to about 23—all in one fell swoop. His argument is, you can understand what happened to the country in the sixties when you understand that fact.

It is a cliché to say that baby boomers are essentially more liberal on social and cultural matters and more conservative on economic issues, but the truth of the matter is, that is what they are, and it has been that way since the early 1970s. Warren Miller did some very important work in his book *Leadership and Change* in 1975, in which he looked at this generation and said, "Lo and behold, this is really going to be quite different." One of his points was how anti–New Deal the attitudes of the baby boomers were—anti–New Deal in terms of their suspicion of the size of government and of government solutions to economic problems. By the way, this preceded the huge inflation in oil prices and stagflation. It partly had to do with a philosophy, as Lee pointed out, of "anti-bigness." It had to do with a discomfiting feeling about the government, and a yearning for individual success. At the same time Miller found, of course, that they were far more liberal on cultural matters, social matters, and issues like the environment.

It was his thesis at the time that this presaged an enormous, potentially different but still liberal, majority in the country—but not liberal in the traditional sense.

What has been happening since is that the Democratic party

seems to have had a death wish to drive this generation away from it. The Republican party has cleverly masked some of its problems, but neither party has come to grips with how to seize this majority. There is a danger in appealing to the baby boom. It has been written about by Mike Barone, who speculated some months ago that maybe this is a generation that will go down in history as having totally altered the social and cultural context of its society and never once attained political power. The baby-boom generation may get outmaneuvered by an alliance between those ahead of it and those behind it because of its size and because it is in fact unique. And that is a problem for someone who's appealing to this generation—how to do so without alienating older and younger voters. Interestingly, people under 25 now look like they have more in common with people of 45 than they do with people who are between 25 and 40, and thank God there are so few of them. That's for all of you who never liked your younger brothers and sisters—now you understand why.

So the big events that have shaped this generation have all had to do with change: the role of women, race, self-actualization, and Vietnam.

Another important characteristic, and one that goes back to Vietnam, is the anti-establishment nature of the baby-boom generation. It does not like the establishment. It never did like it, and, as I pointed out, I thought the cruel irony of 1984 was that there was an effort to restore the status quo ante 1968, if you will, by labor and other forces in the Democratic party. You can see it in the protégés of the leaders of 1968, including Martin Luther King, and there's rich irony in the fact that the Democratic party would attempt to impose the status quo ante 1968—in the person of Hubert Humphrey's protégé—on this generation of the street demonstrations. And they wonder why 34 percent of Gary Hart's voters voted for Ronald Reagan? As I said to the Democratic Senate caucus, "Remember, this generation—particularly its liberal elements—was in the streets against this party for much of its youth."

The baby-boom generation has no real personal affinity for the party, and so when it reacts to the party establishment, it is saying something symbolic. It's interesting to me that Reagan's lead over Mondale and Hart during most of the spring of 1984 was in the marginal range until June—on average about 5 or 6 percent against Mondale and about 1 to 2 percent against Hart. In June, when it became clear that Mondale would be the Democratic nominee, the

44

bottom fell out. The margin rose to 15 points. Reagan's lead came essentially from baby boomers, who looked at the Mondale nomination and said, "If that's what they're really going to do, goodbye." And they just left, in droves.

Let me elaborate a bit on the cultural and technological changes that have taken place in society. Besides being huge and self-contained, this generation also has television. All of a sudden television is a homogeneous experience that allows the child growing up in Mississippi, the child growing up in New York, and the child growing up in California to experience for the first time all the same images and information. And that's why the Davy Crockett hats and the hula hoops are everywhere, not just in particular places.

And so the geographic division of American politics and American life begins to diminish—all because of the power of television. And these are the children of television and technology. It is not surprising that their byword—traditional in America anyway, but they've taken it to an extreme—is "change." They love change. America is about change; it always has been. The party that has been about change has always been the dominant party in this country.

As we get into politics, the other point I want to make about the baby boomers is how very *late* they experience everything. It is, again, the advantage of being self-contained and being so big. Baby boomers think the world was made for them. That's the way they've always been treated. We did have wealth and luxury in that sense, compared with our parents, and we've had the luxury of thinking about things other than how we're going to get by. So we have been late, and you can see this in two areas.

One is families. Look at the surge in the birth rate for older baby boomers, to people over 35. A lot of baby boomers got married late, had children late, and are buying homes late, compared with other generations. This lateness means that there is a delayed impact when these experiences finally occur.

The other thing that they've been late to, of course, is politics, which is partly a function of their being anti-establishment and of their reaction to the political system in general. They have still not had their full impact. It was clear by 1983 that you were seeing the first signs of real political activity on the part of these young people. Actually, you could see it in 1980, in the dichotomy of John Anderson's support, which was liberal on social/cultural issues and much more conservative economically. Anderson did much better among independents and young voters and in the suburbs.

All through 1982 and 1983 you could see it among young blacks, who were the people responsible for electing Harold Washington in Chicago and Wilson Goode in Philadelphia. It was not older blacks who made those people mayor; it was blacks under age 35 pouring into the political process—voting as opposed to being in the streets, which is where a lot of people thought they'd be in reaction to the Reagan administration. So the baby boomers have been late, but they entered the picture in 1984 and Gary Hart was able to reach them, to really strike a chord with them, and we got the most enormous eruption in American politics.

Understand that Gary Hart, in the several weeks after New Hampshire, gained more ground in both the nomination and general election campaigning—when measured in public polls—than anyone had ever done in such a short time. It took Jimmy Carter and George McGovern four or five months to accomplish what Gary Hart was able to do in essentially three weeks. It was a result of the velocity of the movement on the part of the baby-boom generation. You can learn a lot from the reaction of both parties to this phenomenon.

The White House, as I understand it, panicked in reaction to Gary Hart's rise. Hart's was the kind of candidacy that you would least want if you were a Republican strategist with a president who was popular but in his seventies. It would mean an election in which the campaign could be about the future, not Reagan's best ground because he would not be the central figure necessarily. To the Republicans' credit, they spent enormous amounts of money on studies and strategies asking, "What are we going to do about this? How are we going to get hold of these voters?"

The Democratic response is most interesting. It is happening in *their* party, and this is why I said, see the ghosts of 1968. What is the reaction of the Establishment of the Democratic party? It is to pretend the baby boom doesn't exist, to drive it out as much as possible. Look at the Democratic convention if you want to understand its political reaction to the baby boom. We have a certain nominee, Walter Mondale, who is having trouble—"trouble" is a kind word—with these voters. You can see the data in June. Now, since you have established your party base, you would think you would use your convention to reach out to these voters, right?

Wrong. And it wasn't that they didn't think about it. It was placed on the table, and it was rejected.

If you look at the speakers who addressed the Democratic convention during prime time—and there were some very great speeches given—you will discover that none of the party's younger stars appeared except Chris Dodd, and he got to appear because Gary Hart picked him to nominate him. The younger stars—the Bradleys, the Bidens, the Babbitts—never appeared on the convention platform at all. Now that's a real statement. That's called wooden-headedness, that's what Barbara Tuchman wrote about in *The March of Folly*.

What happened in this election is overwhelming. Up until 1980, the Democrats did best with men and with younger voters. Even in 1980 they carried the youngest cohort in the election. But in 1984 not only did the Democrats not carry them, they didn't even run better with them than with other voters. The universe flipped over, and Reagan walked off with the baby boomers and younger voters, by massive percentages.

And yet the baby boomers saved the Democratic party in the Congress. If you look at the House races nationally, according to the ABC breakdown, which is more precise along generational lines, you find that the Democrats barely broke even with voters under 25, lost the age-groups over 40, and carried only the baby boomers. Look at the defections from the Democratic party, whether blue-collar, labor, college-educated, or whatever, and you see that it was not with the older cohorts that the Democrats lost ground; it was with voters under 40. Baby-boom defections to the Republican side were massive. It was with the lower-age half of every one of these groups that the Republicans made real gains for Reagan, and it looks like they made potential gains for the future.

Now in the face of that you would expect the Democratic party to say, "That's what we have to deal with." Instead, the Democrats, first of all, want to say it's a regional problem—the whites in the South. But they got only 31 percent of the whites in the industrial Midwest, compared with 27 percent in the South, so it's hard to see how it could be a "regional" problem. They also say the problem is ideological, that Democrats aren't conservative enough. But when you lose 43 percent of white liberals to Ronald Reagan, you have a problem that extends beyond ideology. In hard numbers, it is a problem of the defection of the base vote of the Democratic party.

Except for Mondale, who has pointed out the problem, not one major spokesman has talked about the generational problem with the baby boom. The reason is very simple: it is easier to say one is out of step than to say one is passé. And for the leadership of the Democratic party to admit that the problem is generational is to say that their time is over. People do not yield power easily. If you don't believe that, look at the British Labour party. And that is the problem with the Democratic party right now.

The Democrats should be better able to appeal to this generation than the Republicans. The thing that most concerned the Republicans in the general election was how the Mondale campaign would do if it finally did get around to dealing with Jerry Falwell and the danger of the social issues with baby-boom voters. The Republican convention had been a disaster in that sense, had given the Democrats a great opening they did not exploit. Reagan gained less from the Dallas convention than Hubert Humphrey did from his convention in 1968 because of what appeared on that television set: too much of the religious right. And yet the Democrats didn't exploit that. Instead, the Mondale staff insisted it was going to run on the economics of the deficit and on tax increases and came pouring out of the trenches to the likely result, in the face of what was the flank opportunity and one of the great historic strategic moves of our time in American politics.

So the Republican party's vulnerability is its right wing. The Democrats' difficulty is the problem of shedding the New Deal. Can they once again be the party of change? The Jack Kemps and others are insisting that the Republicans be the party of change. (And I assume there's a reason behind Jack Kemp's moving to the left on social issues.) The question is, can the Democrats take advantage of this opportunity?

My last point is this: neither party has a claim on the baby-boom generation yet. This generation is basically probably more liberal than conservative. But it doesn't really matter; those terms are irrelevant. Lee Atwater got to the heart of the problem: these are people—this is a generation—with a collective social conscience, a collective sense that they can do great things, yet they are leading a life right now that's fairly mundane (even if they like their lifestyles) in terms of changing the world. This is a generation that grew up believing it was going to reshape the world, and that's where its power is. Neither political party has been able to reach this generation in a way that would allow it—and its aspiration to change the world—to become a central power force. Which leads to the real question for 1988 and beyond: which party, if either, is going to be able to accomplish that? The one that does will likely be the majority party for the rest of the century.

John Fund, *Wall Street Journal: If candidates are going to have to appeal to baby-boom voters by breaking out of some of the orthodoxies of their parties, it's pretty clear, for Republicans, that if a Republican moves left on social issues, some of the leaders of the New Right are going to become very upset very quickly. Likewise, for the Democrats, if you appeal to the baby boomers' economic aspirations and lack of allegiance to the New Deal, obviously the labor leaders and others are going to object strongly. At what point do you start losing voters as you appeal to the baby boom?*

Atwater: First of all, someone told me that when I appeared here today with Pat I wouldn't have to say a single bad word about the Democrats; he would take care of it. Thanks, Pat.

In answering your question, I think the first thing you need to look at as a Republican strategist is, what are the things that unify libertarians/baby boomers with the populist/social-issue voters? Number one, consider the notion of individualism. Look at the average populist voter, the Northern ethnic and the Southern white. They consider themselves strong individuals, and so do baby boomers. Also, consider the anti-establishment theme. If you go back and study the Populist movement from the 1890s to the present, you find a strong strain of anti-establishment feeling. I agree with Pat 100 percent on the anti-establishment orientation of the baby boomers. The anti–big institution, anti–big government feeling is another unifying theme. So you have to start by appealing to those unifying themes in the two groups.

Second, if you're a Republican strategist, your job is not to try to reeducate populists on what they should believe about social issues, but rather to concentrate on the notion of tolerance. One of the things Reagan did so well was that he often took very conservative positions on social issues, but at the same time he was able to establish the fact that he was a tolerant man. That's basically the approach you have to take on social issues.

Also, you can use economic issues as unifying themes. Baby boomers are much more concerned with economic issues than they are with social issues. It is only when they think that social structures and social issues are being dictated to them that they actually

49

get turned off enough to vote against someone on the basis of social issues.

Caddell: Let me just say that I didn't want to leave the impression that I could trash the Democratic party alone. Let me try Lee's party for a moment and even up the score here.

Atwater: I shouldn't have said that, Pat.

Caddell: You really shouldn't have, Lee. First of all, I think the Republicans have an inherent problem that they're glossing over. They're talking about it in terms of a "tolerance problem." But I think it's going to be very difficult to keep telling the Jerry Falwells and the Pat Robertsons to deliver their votes while continuing to tell them you're not going to raise their social agenda. The social issues will really come to the fore politically for the Democrats when the Supreme Court begins to move on social issues. If you start tampering with the *Roe* v. *Wade* abortion decision, you threaten an entire generation of women who believe that abortion is their right. If you want to see political activism, you will see it then. That's why, from a tactical perspective, I have always wanted to see the Human Life Amendment brought to the floor of Congress. I understood why the White House was trying to suppress it during the last administration. They're going to have a hard time dealing with the problem of telling these people, as we told a lot of groups in the Democratic party for years, "Hey, we understand what you want, but we can't give it to you because we'll lose votes. You keep waiting, and someday we'll deliver." Sooner or later, they're going to demand that their loyalty and support be rewarded in terms of public policy. And when that moment comes, that's when you'll start striking political sparks because when you threaten people, they begin to react politically.

It seems to me that the Republicans have a potentially even greater problem. If the Democratic party can stop being bogged down as the party of the status quo and the representative of institutional leaders rather than of the constituencies of those institutions, then the Republicans have a problem. The Republican message in Dallas, it seemed to me, was "You're on your own." It's every man for himself—not every woman, either. That seems to me to run against the latent social consciousness of the generation

Lee talked about, which is one of a sense of community and togeth-
erness and yet in that framework of individualism.

Now, on the issue of how the Democrats should craft their appeal
to the baby-boom generation without losing the rest of the voters,
it seems to me that it has to restore the idea that it is the party of
economic growth, which is its traditional appeal to older voters and
to blue-collar workers, and that in this context it is willing to support
individualism. And yet, at the same time, it must show it is willing
to ensure that this society move together. I don't think the Democrats have as far to go in the long term—they have a much more
emotional move to make right now, and I'm not sure they can make
it because, as I said, it's about power—but still they have an easier
road in the long term than do the Republicans. The Republicans,
however, are bringing to bear a greater intelligence, if you will, and
a greater understanding of opportunity than the Democrats.

Phil Kellett, National Treasury Employees Union: *Mr. Atwater,
you talked about these new values that the baby-boom generation possesses,
and you talked about self-actualization being a good descriptive term for
them. Would you equate self-actualization with self-determination?*

*Mr. Caddell, if you were asked to advise labor organizations on how to
relate to the baby-boom generation, what would you say?*

Atwater: Yes, to a certain extent I would equate self-actualization
with self-determination. I would also equate it with the idea of
individual freedom, of individualism, which is one of the values
particularly developed in the sixties. You find that there are a lot of
new values that are basically personal values.

Caddell: The labor unions have enormous opportunities if they
will grasp them. I thought the recent AFL-CIO meeting offered both
the most positive and the most distressing signals. I hope some of
the rhetoric that came out of the meeting, that which analyzed the
past, was simply a reflection of internal politics and not of the
union's real beliefs. On the other hand, it seemed to me that the
study the labor unions did on their future was a terrific picture of
where they have to go. Labor unions have a lot of baby-boom
members, but what they have to do is adapt the way unions are
run to the cultural and social individualism of this generation, while
remembering that community is important. A number of people in

51

this generation are finding themselves stuck because high tech is not quite the paradise that was promised.

Yes, there are lots of yuppies. But there are lots and lots of people—men and women, particularly women—who are in the service economy, who are well educated, who find themselves sitting in front of computers punching in insurance data all day long for wages that are substantially less than what men earn in other areas. The high-tech revolution is going to make a few people very rich and very happy, and a lot of people are going to find it drudgery, and that offers an opportunity for the trade-union movement.

But for a union to act in a dictatorial fashion, to presume that it can speak for its members, will keep those people from unionizing. There's got to be a socialization process, and if there is, there's a real future for a transformed trade-union movement in this country.

But let me return to the Republicans for a minute. When I listen to David's recommendation that the Republicans keep their economic conservatism and become more tolerant, or more liberal, on social and cultural matters, it strikes me that what we're asking the Republican party to become is the Rockefeller liberal Republican party again. And you all remember how popular that was with the conservatives. But if you think about it, that's where that road leads. You could perhaps call it "Rockefeller Republicanism" without its establishment base.

Atwater: Well, Pat, as a southern Republican who worked for Strom Thurmond for nine years, I would say, rather than Rockefeller liberalism—*populism*. You need to maintain a strain of populism in dealing with the whole spectrum of issues.

Boaz: Let me respond here to the suggestion that I'm recommending some kind of Rockefeller Republicanism. To begin with, the Establishment element *is* Rockefeller Republicanism. I'm not sure you can have Rockefeller Republicanism that isn't Establishment. But also, while I think that this sort of socially tolerant, economically conservative approach could be appealing to the remaining number of Republican moderates—the John Anderson vote, those sorts of people—I do think that to appeal to the younger voters a Jack Kemp sort of approach to the economy makes more sense than the old Rockefeller style. It's not the same thing. It should be an upbeat, high-tech, future-oriented kind of economic conservatism, not the economic conservatism of Rockefeller (to the extent that that's a fair term) or even of some of the southern Republicans who sometimes do not seem very future-oriented in their conservatism.

Caddell: Well, David, what I would then argue is, I wasn't thinking of Rockefeller in terms of his economics. I was really thinking of Rockefeller in terms of his social liberalism—on civil rights, on race, on women, and so on. That's what I find the greatest rub with some of the southern populists in the Republican party.

Boaz: For the last 20 years, certainly, the Republican party has been trending away from this kind of approach, but there's a new constituency that might be available to the Republicans if they reoriented their approach. And Lee is probably right in saying that the best way to do that is not to say, "We're socially liberal," but simply not to talk about social issues—but if the Supreme Court becomes active, you can't do that.

Caddell: Right. That's where the tensions come in.

I do believe this move on blacks is very smart. If the Republicans are smart and keep pushing economics, and if the Democrats let them do it, the Republicans are going to end up winning sizable black support in future years on economic issues. A lot of young blacks—if you look at the Jesse Jackson vote—would not have voted for Mondale if Jackson had not been in the race. You wouldn't have known this, of course, from the kind of simplistic reporting that the press gave us, which we've all come to love and cherish, along with their definition of ideology. The truth is, those Jesse Jackson blacks were the same young blacks in Philadelphia and Chicago who were electing Goode and Washington, and they are really different from older blacks. On economic issues they're very unhappy with what they believe is the inability of big government to deliver. So you can make a case for economic individualism and for entrepreneurialism.

There are black voters who should be Democrats, who will listen to that message; and if it is a choice between continuing the way it's been going with big government or cutting it all out, they'll stay with big government. But if the choice is one between staying with big government—all the social welfare programs, and no hope—

and some really interesting approaches and individual efforts, a lot of these people are going to vote for Republicans.

Don Haroz, Prudential Capital Management International: *How do you think the baby boomers will feel about the issue of free trade?*

Caddell: I think the answer to that question is unclear. Young voters are not interested in protectionism. First of all, they have a much greater world view. As I discovered in the primaries, they're not as interested in protectionism simply to preserve dying industries or industries that won't help themselves. On the other hand, and this is where it gets complicated, these people have a notion about excellence and being number one, and competing. If they believe that the United States is being treated unfairly, they're going to be like other Americans: they're going to respond to it.

Boaz: Bill Schneider was right this morning: this is basically an elite vs. popular position. You've got a pretty high percentage of the average voters in any ideological group being in favor of protectionism instinctively, at least since World War II, and yet that whole time you've seen virtual unanimity among elites for free trade. But in recent years we've seen a shift among American labor leaders, who used to be reasonably free-trade. We're seeing more of a shift among businessmen these days. The automobile industry used to be free-trade. Now, it may be that there's no ideology involved here; it's just that inefficient industries decide they need protection. My guess, based on the polls I've seen, is that the baby-boom voters would be less supportive of protectionism than other groups, but that you can probably still find a majority of them in favor of it. So far, there haven't been elites willing to lead the protectionist effort, and as long as that continues to be the case we probably won't get stuck with a protectionist policy. But I think you would see support for it if you had the right leadership.

Atwater: I feel very strongly that in the long haul—sometime before the year 2000—you will find a solid popular consensus on the free-trade side just because of the world view of this group and because of the changes in the economy and technology. One of the major changes this group will make in American political thought, probably in the next 10 or 15 years, will be in stimulating a decidedly free-trade outlook.

54

Diane Thompson, National Organization for Women: *Each of the panelists has identified the changing role of women and the integration of women into the work force as significant factors affecting the baby boom. Perhaps you could define how these factors have affected the baby boom and also how what we hope will be their continuation affects your predictions for the future and the continuing political activity of that group.*

Caddell: The impact is fairly great because it's a social impact. There's real division between baby-boom women and older women over the role of women in work and society. I think that baby-boom men are more tolerant than older men about it, although there is still difficulty with the older baby boomers, a generation of men that have been forced to change. The Mondale campaign found that younger men were more interested in a woman candidate for vice president than were any other group in the electorate other than young women. That was mentioned to me at the time of the convention, and I thought it was a dangerous kind of interpretation because it seemed to me that maybe people just don't want to admit their antipathy toward a woman.

I think it's interesting that the greatest reaction against the Ferraro nomination politically came from young men, even though the youngest men in the electorate, who have grown up with equality, are in fact the most supportive intellectually and attitudinally of an equal role in society for women. They have the least problem with it in the abstract because they've grown up with it. What was interesting about these young men wasn't that they were anti-women; it was that they were trying to find some way of expressing themselves because in fact they'd been relatively ignored, and they're the first group of men to face that problem for a long time. That's why there was so much "John Wayne macho." There was a lot of cultural feeling there about expression, about finding their place.

Basic support for the movement of women as equals in society and in the work force is very real, and it will continue because a new generation is entering society that has lived through it. The baby boomers are grappling with it, and for them it will not come overnight, but it will come. It depends, however, on what kind of women's movement evolves. A women's movement that is extremist or tends to look extremist is going to incite those men to react. But the trend of history is clear.

Atwater: I think the extremist brand of liberalism in the women's movement will be eradicated by the baby-boom movement. One of the things that happened in 1984 was the beginning of the end for the extreme feminist movement. Not only will NOW endorsements not be sought after by candidates in the future, candidates will probably try to frame opponents to get NOW endorsements.

But there is a women's movement that's very powerful in this country, and it will continue. As Pat said about the older leadership in the Democratic party, the Bella Abzug–type leadership will be moved out of the women's movement relatively quickly, and it will be done by women of the baby boom.

What is happening in the workplace in the long term is an integration of values. In other words, you find women getting more and more competitive, getting values that were traditionally male workplace values, but at the same time you find men becoming more sensitive to things that were traditionally associated with female values. The baby boom will usher in a new kind of person with hybrid values, the new synthesis. It will be interesting to see how it plays out in the end, politically. From the standpoint of my party, we need to get in the forefront of equal pay and issues like that.

Caddell: It is workplace issues that are important, and also political power. To some extent, the Republicans are actually having an easier time of it than the Democrats. But the real issue—women and political power—is going to be critical for the Democrats. The Democratic party is the party that is all male-led, and yet a majority of its voters right now are female. How it adapts to that without looking like it has gone off the deep end is a problem.

Boaz: I was struck by the number of people who told me last fall that the ticket they'd really like to vote for was Reagan/Ferraro. In a sense, that is a libertarian, baby-boom kind of impulse. They wanted Reagan's economic policy, but they liked the image of Ferraro—reasonably young, new to politics, a symbol of social change that was important. That would have been an interesting kind of approach. It may very well be that the next opportunity to vote for a woman for national office will come from the Republican side.

I was also struck by the number of newspaper articles about women who were for Reagan who said, "Well, of course I don't agree with him on ERA and abortion, but I think the economic issues are more important." You saw a lot of that among young businesswomen. To some extent, this is the way the Republican party may get around the social-issue problem: for the last 15 years people haven't really felt their social freedoms were threatened. Even on issues like drugs, the laws are still on the books, but they're not really enforced against users; abortion has been legal now for 12 years; we don't have ERA, but most people have gotten most of what they wanted from ERA anyway.

The movement of women into the workplace, which comes before political change generally, is the most important social change that we've seen in the last 20 or 25 years. And it is an area where conservatives aren't necessarily ready to accommodate. To some extent all the talk about family and traditional values—explicitly in the case of someone like George Gilder, more implicitly in the general conservative rhetoric—indicates a hostility toward women's new role in society.

We've talked about America being a country of change, and we're seeing today that liberals are not very positive toward economic change. Liberal programs include plant-closing restrictions, protectionism, shoring up smokestack industries—all of them attempts to prevent change. By the same token, a lot of conservative programs represent resistance to social change—"traditional values," "restore the family," "restore moral decency," and so on. So the winning party in the future may be the one that is able to better accommodate change.

Martin Wooster, *Harper's: The parties seem to be switching their historic views on the draft. Jack Kemp, for example, has recently come out four-square against the draft, while neoliberals are toying with various types of national service. Which strategy do you think will appeal to the post–baby-boom generation in the long run?*

Atwater: That can be answered very quickly. As long as the United States is not immediately threatened, young people are going to oppose the draft.

Caddell: The problem with national service is economics. This is the generation, obviously, of the Peace Corps and groups like that; there is some appeal to it. Coercion is another problem. But it depends on the environment we're in—not only the immediate threat militarily, but also whether there's a consensus in society, an appeal to revitalization. In that context, national service in a broader form can have some appeal, particularly because the baby boom won't have to go this time.

On the other hand, if that consensus doesn't exist, you run right into a political problem. The element of coercion—people's feeling about it—runs very much counter to our tradition of individual liberty. So it's an issue that's not yet resolved because it depends on what kind of context it's put in. If national service is limited simply to the draft, you can kiss that one goodbye.

Boaz: As I mentioned in my talk, one of the problems with this issue is that at any given moment a draft or national service is discussed, everybody who can vote is already exempt from it. And that does make a difference. Nevertheless, I think people feel that it would be very divisive, and that's going to keep politicians from wanting to implement it. You saw that in 1980 when Carter was looking for ways to "get tough." He was willing to go for draft registration, but he wouldn't have wanted to go beyond that. Any president is going to worry about a new campus revolt if the draft is reinstated.

Caddell: Well, that would be one way of testing the reality of the new conservatism on college campuses, I suppose. We would get a real quick answer to how gung ho today's students really are. Lee, I think you should go to the White House and make that suggestion. I think we should try it out.

III. The View from Congress

Rep. Vin Weber: We are moving in a very general way toward the idea of less government, lower taxes, and less regulation—not that people generally accept every iota of the Reagan program, but the old linkage of activist government–better times–Democrat is rapidly becoming less government–better times–Republican. And unless that can be turned around, it is going to be very difficult for the Democratic party to halt the process of realignment that is taking place.

There are other issues that complicate the picture somewhat. National defense and foreign policy are, of course, complicating factors. It's interesting to me that the Democrats seem to be making national defense and foreign policy the major issues in this particular biennium—aid to the *contras*, the MX missile, and reductions in the defense budget. And on any one of those issues they certainly find that a majority of the people, according to the polls, are backing them up. Nonetheless, polls from the last election show that almost 50 percent of the Democrats who voted for Reagan did so because they think the Democrats are soft on national defense—again, not at a specific programmatic level but at a symbolic and general level. I would argue strongly that although people may take positions of a dovish nature on specific and narrow defense and foreign policy issues, when it comes to actual voting behavior, people seem to almost always fear that one party or one candidate is too soft.

Finally, there are the issues that I suppose present the greatest challenge to our party, issues that may be called traditional values, family values, or moral issues. They present us with a significant challenge as Republicans.

First of all, in my judgment the most significant political movement in the country today is the movement of evangelical and fundamentalist Christians into the political process. That is not my background—I am a Catholic—but there is no question that in Minnesota and in some of the southern states that's the most significant political movement today. The Nielsen ratings say that 60 million Americans now regularly watch the Christian Broadcasting

Network. The Gallup Poll says that 45 percent of all Americans watch a weekly religious broadcast, and in my state we were shocked to find, according to the Minnesota poll, that 36 percent of Minnesotans consider themselves "born-again Christians."

That is a lot of people. They are not an organized political force, but they are coming into the political process with an agenda that has not been addressed by either party for a long, long time. They are coming into it increasingly in the Republican party because of President Reagan's leadership.

That challenges us because the under-35 voting group probably contains the largest number of social libertarians—who may at some future date rebel against a party that takes what they consider a restrictive stance on social liberty. Nonetheless, for the time being the reality of the votes, as opposed to theories about the behavior of young voters, suggests that the movement of the evangelical Christians into politics has accrued substantially to the net benefit of the Republican party, and unless there is a reaction among younger voters in the near future, they will continue to accrue to the benefit of the Republican party.

My guess is that we *are* living in a period of realignment. Even if I didn't believe that, I would probably say so.

Rep. Tim Wirth: I was reelected in my suburban Denver district in 1982 with about 63 percent of the vote. At nine o'clock on election night 1984 we were looking at the numbers and hoping that the vote in Boulder County, where the University of Colorado is located, would come in as strong as it had before because otherwise we might well go down the chute.

In the state of Colorado we ended up with a veto-proof Republican legislature and overwhelming Democratic defeat everywhere. The best candidates the Democratic party has run in the 10 years that I've been involved—those running for county commissioner and for the state legislature—got wiped out uniformly. It was an absolute disaster. My wife and I boarded an airplane the following Friday, arrived in Washington at about two o'clock, and I went to a meeting in the speaker's office at about four o'clock where Speaker O'Neill and Majority Leader Jim Wright told the Steering and Policy Committee of the Democratic party how great the 1984 election had been. We had picked up two seats in the Senate, and had lost only a handful of seats in the House, despite this overwhelming Reagan "mandate," so we'd done very well indeed. I went home feeling as if I were in a completely different world from the one in which I had been campaigning for the previous three months.

We can see that it was an overwhelming shift. The President carried 49 states. Over the last 20 years the Republican party has won some 65 percent of the electoral vote, so on the one hand the Democrats are truly in very deep trouble. On the other hand, a vast majority of the governors in the country are Democrats, we Democrats control most state legislatures, and, maybe most importantly, in 1984 we won some 65 percent of the contested elections across the country.

You can argue that there is a fundamental realignment going on with Ronald Reagan, and you can point to demographics that either prove or disprove it. The most important phenomenon, it seems to me, is the fact that Reagan thoroughly dominates the American political landscape. But that is not going to continue through 1988 and cause a real realignment because Reagan, like other presidents, will be looking for his place in history.

His place in history is not in the realignment of the Republican party, nor is it over on the far right. His place is, as most presidents know, somewhere in the center. His place in American history will be focused predominantly on arms control and the relationship of the United States with the Soviet Union, and that's how he's going to define his remaining time in office.

So what does all of this tell us? Not a lot. What we do know, however, is that both parties are changing very significantly, particularly the younger leadership in the parties. At the senior level, Reagan is not going to run again, and people tend to forget that. He is becoming more of a lame duck with each passing day—an important consideration for the Democratic party.

Maybe from my perspective one of the joys of 1984 is that neither Reagan nor Mondale will run again. The Democrats learned a very bitter lesson in 1984, and that's that the American people would rather be rich than poor and that the Mondale proposal for higher taxes was not the kind of politics the country's looking for or that most sensible politicians would have pursued.

More interesting, I think, is what's happening with the congressional leadership. You see a changing of the guard, particularly in the House of Representatives, where the most interesting ideas come from people of the generation between, say, 35 and 50, who've been in the House anywhere from zero to 12 years—the "middle management" group, one would say. I would certainly include Vin

Weber in that group among the Republicans, as well as Newt Gingrich, Jack Kemp, and an array of people with whom one can violently disagree but at least have a spirited exchange of ideas because their ideas have some substance.

I would hope that the Republicans would say that there is some substance on our side as well. I'm talking about people who have thought through what they want their party to be, why they're in the Congress, and where they want to go. The sole purpose of many people who dominated the House in the past was, it seemed, to get reelected rather than to carry forward a set of ideas and a set of ideals. I would hope that such a generational shift is obvious in the Democratic party as well.

Who's going to win this battle? It will, of course, be determined partly by variables over which we have no control, but there are a couple of themes that are terribly important for my party to think about, and I'm sure that the Republicans are thinking about them as well. One of them is, who controls the center? The second is, who defines the role of the federal government? As for the first, we have had a tension in the United States for 200 years—a tension between equality and excellence, between a Jeffersonian theme and a Hamiltonian theme, between opportunity and economic growth. There's nothing wrong with that; they're mutually exclusive at times, battling each other at times—nothing new about it at all in our history. Successful politicians in the United States are those who weave together the two themes of opportunity and excellence, growth and equality.

Whoever puts those two themes together will determine who controls the center. It's not going to be done on the far right or on the far left, as we have discovered. The peril for the Republicans is that there may be an enormous amount of ideology on the far right that is driving them. We Democrats learned our lesson, and we're coming back to the center, for there's extraordinary opportunity for the Democratic party to reclaim the dynamism of that center in the United States.

The second issue that is going to determine, in terms of ideas, who controls that center and who wins is the issue of defining the federal government. I don't think that this issue is defined, as some of our conservative brethren would suggest, in terms of a central government or an activist government. I don't think those are the themes that drive Americans in thinking about their government; rather, it's who defines that partnership between the public and

62

the private sector for the remainder of this decade and who best reflects our history.

That history is one in which the public and the private have cooperated since the mercantilist era—the canals, the land-grant universities, the railroads, the space program, the highway program, or any number of initiatives involving precisely that kind of cooperation between the public and private sectors. Defining that relationship will be one of the dominant themes that will determine who wins control of our government over the remainder of this century.

I don't think we learned very much from 1984; the jury is still very much out. There is clearly a very strong generation of new people coming up who are trying to define how to win. Winning will depend on who defines the center, and that definition will be expressed in terms of our understanding of those two conflicting themes in America—Jeffersonian and Hamiltonian. In other words, winning will depend on who defines the relationship between the public and private sectors.

Question: *Was the 1984 election primarily a personal victory for Ronald Reagan rather than a conservative mandate?*

Weber: I'm really sorry that the Reagan campaign consciously decided to avoid a real debate on the issues in 1984. They wanted to avoid issues; they wanted to run a symbolic, image-wise campaign. Who knows how it would have worked out if they'd decided to join the intellectual debate? My feeling, since I am basically an optimist, is that although he might not have carried 49 states, being from Minnesota, that doesn't bother me at all. We might have done somewhat better at the lower levels of government because there might have been a connection between party voting and the presidential ticket. I basically think that my party and philosophy are on the ascendant, so I wish that the president had joined the debate more thoroughly.

It was a terrible mistake that our party decided to follow a strategy based on image. We got an inkling of the power an intellectual debate could have from Gary Hart's campaign. I'm not going to suggest that he had an opportunity to flesh out his ideas and really join in the debate, either with Mondale or Reagan, but he basically came within an eyelash of capturing the nomination, based on two words: new ideas.

I am not as cynical as many of my Republican friends, who said that Hart didn't have any new ideas. Hart is about as creative as most people in elected political office are, coming from his own philosophical vantage point. Politicians are brokers of ideas, compromisers of ideas, purveyors of ideas; they don't originate them.

But Hart was as good as anybody in trying to initiate a debate, and he went a long way by doing so. I think a debate has to happen—I hope it happens—in the 1988 campaign. That's one of the reasons, I think, that Kemp would be a better candidate for the Republicans than Bush, although I think the vice president is a fine person. But Kemp is better able to carry forward the campaign if it becomes a debate of ideas.

Question: *Can the religious right and the younger, more libertarian voters be brought together in one party?*

Weber: They definitely can be brought together. You know, the coalition that has been the Democratic party for most of the last 50 years has certainly contained contradictions at least as great as those between evangelical and fundamentalist voters, on the one hand, and young, socially libertarian voters, on the other. The fact is, until 1968 we had George Wallace and Martin Luther King in the same party. We had northern labor-union leaders and southern union busters. There's nothing wrong with that; we have a centrist party structure in this country, and any governing coalition is going to contain some contradictions. Managing those contradictions and conflicts is the challenge of the majority party.

How can we manage it? It's not hard to figure out what we should do from a simple vote-getting standpoint. People may be divided on various issues, but people don't vote in a divided way. What matters to us as politicians—at the crass, electoral level—is not what people think about issues but what issues cause them to vote.

What has happened in the last few elections is that people who are conservative on social, moral, or lifestyle issues have voted on the basis of those issues; people who are liberal or libertarian on those issues generally have not. The liberals and libertarians who did vote on that basis are firmly entrenched in the Democratic party anyway. So up to now it hasn't been a real problem.

Wirth: I think this conflict is going to prove to be an enormous problem for the Republican party and an enormous opportunity for the Democratic party. If you compare the young, upwardly mobile, better-educated Gary Hart voter with the born-again voter, you find that they are mutually exclusive.

And if you talk to younger individuals about what they want in this country, they say they want a very clear separation between their own beliefs and what their government does. That is much more fundamental than anything else. So it's going to cause the Republicans a very great problem, but it provides the Democrats with, again, a great opportunity to recapture the center. With all due apologies to Vin, who was involved in drafting the 1984 Republican platform, that platform gave us a huge open center. We'll be the majority party for a long time to come, based on that platform.

Question: *What do international trade problems portend for the future politically?*

Weber: We're seeing those problems right now, in agriculture as much as anywhere, and in all the problems that our exporting industries are facing, but the trends that I've been talking about are not just national trends. As a matter of fact, that's one of the reasons I feel somewhat confident in saying that the old connection in voters' minds between government activism and economic prosperity is changing into a general connection between *less* government and prosperity. We see these trends in various forms in Britain, Germany, France, the Third World, and, to a certain extent, in China. Certainly the Pacific rim is a classic example. We've gone through 50 or 75 years in which a statist-oriented approach to the economy has been dominant, and now we're going into a period when a market-oriented approach to the economy will be on the ascendant internationally.

Question: *We've been discussing the idea that the baby-boom generation will be the swing vote in the future and that it tends to be more sympathetic to Democrats on social and foreign policy issues. It's been suggested that if a Democratic candidate for president really became a strong, outspoken advocate of the free market, like Jack Kemp, and maintained a socially liberal outlook and a less militaristic foreign policy, then the Democrats would have a very viable candidate. What do you think?*

Wirth: The Democratic party is going through some extraordinarily unnecessary wringing of hands and beating of breasts. It simply has to go back to basics. The Democratic party is based essentially on two themes of Franklin Roosevelt: one, that we're going to do everything we can to make sure that everybody has a chance to participate in this economy, in this society (and it follows that a whole lot of programs have been pursued); and second, that in order to do this, we're going to do everything we can to expand the economic pie.

What happened during the 1970s was that the Democrats stopped paying attention to the fact that the pie ought to be growing and spent most of their time focusing on how we were going to redistribute the existing economic pie. That got the Democratic party into real trouble. What we have to do now is return to what the party's always been about—both opportunity and growth.

A Democratic candidate should understand and push the themes related to economic growth, not in terms of industrial policy but in terms of the historic partnership between government and the private sector that we've always had in this country. We should carry that into the technologically changing economy and into investments in education.

There are people who want the government to stay out of our personal lives, and there are people who are very skeptical about the role we're playing in the world militarily. Those ingredients—combined with Ronald Reagan no longer being in office and the growing awareness of the huge budget deficit and other problems—means that those chickens have ultimately got to come home to roost. The numbers tell you that.

John Fund, *Wall Street Journal*: *Congressman Wirth represents a district that is more Republican than most districts represented by a Democrat, and Congressman Weber represents a district that is fairly Democratic by most standards. I wonder which issues you two would differ on with a majority of your party's colleagues in the House and whether or not you feel that's been an important factor in your district?*

Weber: I differ somewhat from my party over the environment—and there I do think we have to change or face real serious problems. In the 1960s a consensus emerged in the country that the environment was a major national issue and that the government has to address it. My party doesn't address it very well, particularly in some areas where it should be fairly easy to do so—applying principles of the free market to synthetic-fuel development and nuclear energy, for example. I also think there are some regulatory areas where there should be a more active role for government—a position my party doesn't usually embrace.

Another issue is civil rights. The Republican party cannot be the dominant party for the next generation if we are viewed as the party that, willingly or unwillingly, is the home of bigots. Unfortunately, conservatism has improperly been embraced by bigots in the past for a variety of reasons, and we just have to make it clear that we don't accept that.

Wirth: Isn't it wonderful . . . the battle for the center is under way. Conservative Republicans are worrying about civil rights and the environment. So what has the Democratic party got to do to catch the center?

From the perspective of my district, I would say there are two themes. One is the economic theme I talked about earlier. The people of Colorado, for the most part, don't feel that the Democratic party does a very good job on economic issues. Mine is a high-tech, upwardly mobile, affluent, well-educated district, so there's a big distinction on that front.

There's also a big distinction on what I would call the "idea of governing," or the "process of governance." My district takes the idea of government very seriously. The people there want their government, if it's going to do something, to do it well. They don't perceive right now that the leadership in the Democratic party is governing well and effectively: setting priorities and deciding what it wants to do and what it doesn't want to do.

On both these fronts I believe that our internal organization in the House ought to be much better. Most of my constituents would probably agree. I also believe that there are certain things the Democrats ought to be doing to establish a long-term economic policy; my constituents would probably agree here, too.

IV. Beyond Liberal and Conservative

William B. Lacy, deputy assistant to the president: We are dealing with a totally different political environment now than we were just a few years ago. Things have changed dramatically; it's almost a political equivalent of Alvin Toffler's third wave or John Naisbitt's information age, for we've undergone massive change that faces everyone who analyzes politics.

Some of the most important changes involve the sheer size of politics. If you go back to 1976 and compare it with 1984, you see that something close to a "300 percent rule" is in effect. Committee budgets and staffs on the Republican side have grown by 300 percent. The cost of running a congressional or U.S. Senate race has also grown by 300 percent.

Another change we have witnessed in politics is a tremendous increase in the quantity and quality of information. We have also seen important new technological advances, as well as some very fundamental changes in society that have had an impact on politics and made it very different.

These changes, along with the different philosophical positions we've seen, have really resulted in a change in the way we define the philosophy of politics. The ideological continuum running from right to left is really no longer valid in today's political environment. When you think about the Gary Hart voters who were saying during the primaries that they would vote for Ronald Reagan if Walter Mondale were nominated, or you think about where the yuppies ultimately wound up—strongly supporting the president—or you consider all the changes that we saw among young voters, it's fascinating, and it inspires us to seek some new way to interpret those results. That's what our first speakers on this panel have helped to give us.

Stuart A. Lilie: Bill Maddox and I became interested in this topic as a result of some very casual discussions four or five years ago on the question of what "liberal" and "conservative" meant. We were fascinated by the fact that our peers in academia, the media, and politicians themselves tended to use these terms with some confidence.

But we weren't at all sure, both from an empirical point of view in Bill's work and from a political-philosophy point of view in my work, what these terms actually meant. We were also concerned about a tendency to assume that people need to be placed on the liberal-conservative continuum; if they don't fit as either liberal or conservative, then they are considered to be either inconsistent or not ideological. We wondered whether the people who were labeled "inconsistent" were in fact any more inconsistent than liberals or conservatives.

As we thought about issues in American politics over the last several decades or longer, it occurred to us that there appeared to be at least two enduring issue dimensions. One is the question of economic intervention: what role, if any, should government play in the economy? The other is the question of personal freedom: what are proper and appropriate levels of personal freedom in such areas as free speech, pornography, drugs, sexual practices, and so forth? Most surveys treat these as two distinct dimensions. But then, how can you possibly put them both on a single continuum, which is what the liberal-conservative dichotomy assumes? It assumes that somehow those two dimensions can be blended into one.

So what we did was to use a favorite trick of social scientists: we took those two dimensions and constructed a two-by-two table, as shown in Table 1. To the left on the table is one dimension, "Expansion of Personal Freedoms." That's the wording we used to avoid saying that people were for or against personal freedoms. The other dimension, across the top, is "Government Intervention in Economic Affairs." We dichotomize those two dimensions so that a respondent can be "for" or "against" in each case. And thus we arrived at four ideological types.

Reading across the top, those who support economic intervention but at the same time are for a relatively high level of personal freedoms are labeled "liberal." To the right of that, those who are against government economic intervention but at the same time support high levels of personal freedoms are labeled "libertarian." And in the next row, those who support government economic intervention but also argue for some restrictions on personal freedoms are labeled "populist." And finally, we labeled "conservative" those who are anti-interventionist on economic issues but support some restrictions on personal freedoms.

70

Table 1
ISSUE DIMENSIONS AND IDEOLOGICAL CATEGORIES
PERCENTAGE SUPPORT IN 1980

		Government Intervention in Economic Affairs	
		For	Against
Expansion of Personal Freedoms	For	Liberal 24%	Libertarian 18%
	Against	Populist 26%	Conservative 17%

SOURCE: William S. Maddox and Stuart A. Lilie, *Beyond Liberal and Conservative: Reassessing the Political Spectrum* (Washington: Cato Institute, 1984); Center for Political Studies, University of Michigan.

Based on the 1980 University of Michigan Center for Political Studies survey, we found that 24 percent of those surveyed could be categorized as liberal, 18 percent as libertarian, 26 percent as populist, and 17 percent as conservative. It is interesting to add these figures diagonally. In other words, add the liberals and conservatives together and you'll come up with about 41 percent of the population. Adding the other way and using our new categories of libertarian and populist, you find 44 percent of the population. These numbers suggest that a survey that was looking for only liberals and conservatives would have found almost half the population to be inconsistent or nonideological, and yet, as I would argue, the libertarians and populists are no more inconsistent than liberals or conservatives.

The figures do not add up to 100 percent because we found about 15 percent of the population to be either inattentive or divided. By "inattentive" we mean they didn't answer enough questions to be categorized, and by "divided" we mean that even with our criteria they couldn't be categorized in one of the groups. Nonetheless, 85 percent represents a very high figure for any kind of survey research.

It's important to understand that these categories make some theoretical sense; you can't just take a cluster and say, well, that's an ideology. It must be something other than idiosyncratic, and it must relate to some larger historical and philosophical issues.

The libertarian position is perhaps the most simple and straight-forward, being basically the classical liberalism of the nineteenth century brought forward to the twentieth century. It's a minimal-state position: the state should play a minimal role in all aspects of life, both economic and personal. Basically, the state should be limited to enforcing contracts and maintaining order, domestically and internationally. Thus, in the economic realm the state plays no activist role, and in the realm of personal freedoms people should be allowed to make choices as they see fit. One expression of this idea of personal freedoms that you may be familiar with is the classic essay *On Liberty* by John Stuart Mill, in which Mill basically argues for absolute free speech and for allowing people to do what they want to do, even if it's harmful to themselves, as long as they do not harm others.

The liberal position also came from the nineteenth century, in part as a reaction to some of the conditions of early industrializa-tion—long hours, unsafe working conditions, and so on. Some liberals began to argue that some kinds of economic intervention might be necessary, that in fact to achieve the liberal goal of a free, self-motivating individual, state intervention may be necessary at times to protect against certain kinds of abuses. So in what we call "modern liberalism" there was a tendency to feel that although state intervention is perhaps not good per se, it can have value under certain circumstances. Yet the liberals generally maintain that personal freedoms—questions of censorship, lifestyle, and so on—are essentially not the business of government, and they have maintained a noninterventionist position there.

The conservative position certainly takes the noninterventionist position in economic matters, which I think is very straightforward and doesn't require elaboration, but also argues that there are cer-tain kinds of things that society has a collective wisdom about that individuals do not. Conservatives feel that it is legitimate for society to put certain restrictions on individuals and their behavior to save them from themselves and to save society from them, and that it is therefore legitimate for government to control certain aspects of personal morality.

The populist position shares with the conservative the notion that some kinds of restrictions on personal behavior are legitimate but also holds that economic intervention is necessary at times to protect the "little people" from the abuses of big-business monop-olies and perhaps even from nature itself. In other words, populists feel that government can and should intervene both economically and in the realm of personal freedoms in order to protect individuals.

William S. Maddox: I'd like to focus on one of the simplest ways to look at the implications here, which is to use the four ideological types to talk about the future of the two political parties.

After the 1984 election, of course, we had the quadrennial discussion about where the Democratic party is going to go. After losing four out of the last five presidential elections, Democrats are beginning to ask, "What kind of candidate should we offer? What sort of party should we be?" The Republicans, in turn, are beginning to ask what's going to happen after the Reagan years. What happens after you lose a highly popular president who has kept the ideological battles in the Republican party somewhat minimized for the last few years? One way to approach these questions is to look at the ideological composition of the supporters of the two parties, which is presented in Table 2.

What we're talking about here are party identifiers, that is, people who label themselves Democrats, Republicans, or independents. They are not necessarily party activists or even primary voters. The figures are from 1980, so they're a little dated, but they're the best we have right now.

The Democratic party is composed primarily of populists and liberals, although there are probably fewer populists today than there were in 1980. Populists are a declining group in the electorate. Among the Democrats there are only small segments of conservatives and libertarians. So one major question for the Democratic party now is simply whether it will continue to try to satisfy or somehow reconcile its populist faction (which, by the way, consists largely of blacks and Southern whites and older voters). Or will the Democratic party risk losing some of those populists in an attempt to reach out to independents? The independents, you see, are mostly either liberals or libertarians. In a sense, the Democrats are faced with the problem of deciding whether to hang on to the old to build a coalition, or to try to create some sort of new coalition, realizing that by doing so they may alienate some of the party's standard sources of support.

One possibility for 1988 might be a sort of three-faction race. One faction could be an old-style populist coalition. It could include a majority of blacks, along with some older voters and possibly some

Table 2
IDEOLOGICAL COMPOSITION OF PARTY IDENTIFIERS IN 1980

Democrats	Liberals 30%	Populists 37%	Cons. 11%	Libt. 7%	Divided & Inattentive 15%
Republicans	Liberals 13%	Populists 18%	Conservatives 27%	Libertarians 29%	Divided & Inattentive 13%
Independents	Liberals 25%	Populists 20%	Conservatives 17%	Libertarians 23%	Divided & Inattentive 15%

SOURCE: *Beyond Liberal and Conservative*; Center for Political Studies.

Southern whites—always a very difficult coalition to maintain but one with which many traditional Democrats are comfortable.

A second possibility might be a liberal candidate trying to lead the Democratic core of liberal supporters. You might, in fact, have several candidates battling to provide that leadership for the core liberal vote.

A third possibility might be to have a candidate—either Gary Hart or someone like him—who would draw some support from the core liberal group and also try to bring those liberal or libertarian independents into the Democratic party.

Right now, the Republicans are more divided than we usually assume. The figures show that there are virtually equal numbers of libertarians and conservatives among Republican supporters in the electorate (but who are not necessarily activists), with small segments of both populists and liberals.

So one question for the Republican future, especially for 1988, is whether we will see a repeat of 1980, when five or six candidates were competing for the core conservative element, leaving other Republican voters to base their decisions on personality or some factor other than ideology. The other possibility is that some candidate may step forward with something like a libertarian strategy (though he might not call it that) to attempt to use the libertarian base of Republican supporters as a starting point and draw in libertarian independents to vote in the primaries.

Who might pursue the strategy of attracting libertarian voters? There are several possibilities. Someone could come out of what's usually called the "moderate" or "liberal" wing of the Republican party. Our findings indicate that most of the people usually called "liberal Republicans" are in fact pretty close to being libertarians, as we've defined the category here. You could then have a new face, of course—someone barely known today who could use this strategy to propel himself into serious candidacy. It might also be possible for an old face, maybe one of the well-known Republican candidates—Howard Baker, Bob Dole, or George Bush—to adopt such a strategy. One of those people might consider adopting a new image to separate himself from the other conservative candidates. If some Republican does choose to base his candidacy on the libertarians, you could see a very, very close race for the Republican nomination in 1988—a race that could last all the way to the convention, just like the 1976 Ford and Reagan race.

Michael Barone: I want to begin by congratulating Bill Maddox and Stuart Lilie again on their book, which I think does a nice job of helping to clarify the life of political journalists. There's always a tendency, when you're trying to write something in 200 words or less, to try to use political shorthand and thus over the years the terms "liberal" and "conservative" have been used a great deal. And, as the book points out, these words are really no longer very useful. They cover a wide variety of, I suppose somebody might say, "sins"—of different beliefs—and they don't necessarily mean much anymore.

I found this to be true when I was in the polling business. We'd ask everybody whether they were liberal or conservative or moderate, and we'd then try to figure out what group to go after in order to win the election. We'd then decide we had to go after the moderates, at which point somebody would ask, "Well, do you have a good mailing list of moderates available?" And there are no good mailing lists of moderates.

"Moderate" was not a very useful categorization. One of the reasons, obviously (as the book helps to point out), was that it referred to a wide variety of people. You could have a Democratic congressman from Missouri and a Republican congressman from New York City whose voting records were rated the same by liberal and conservative groups but who voted differently on three out of four roll calls. Both were classified as "moderates," but they were seldom political allies.

Another sign for me that the old labels didn't work came when I looked at some of the polling results from the 1980 Democratic primaries and saw, miraculously, that self-identified liberals, moderates, and conservatives voted in very similar percentages for each of the Democratic candidates. Which is to say that whatever it was that motivated people to vote for a Mondale, a Jesse Jackson, a Gary Hart, an Alan Cranston, or whomever, it was not something that correlated with the labels they gave themselves. Those labels have become obsolete: they pertain to issues of the past, not the politics of today.

This four-box matrix—liberal, libertarian, populist, and conservative—although it's heck to reproduce it in a newspaper article, is very useful for thinking about politics, analyzing elections, and so on. A dozen years ago or more, the typical political analysis, a prime example of which would be Dick Scammon and Ben Wattenberg's book *The Real Majority*, held that the way to win elections and think about who's winning elections is to focus on the center. It was a one-dimensional spectrum, and the voters were all arrayed at different points on a line. Analysts would say, "The fellow who stakes his position closest to the center wins."

Well, that didn't hold very well for the 1980 presidential campaign, in which Jimmy Carter was close to the center and Ronald Reagan was way over to the right. It didn't hold very well even for the 1984 campaign, in which Mondale was probably closer to the center on many issues than Reagan. What makes better sense of the 1984 election is to take the four-box matrix and say that whoever wins three out of four boxes wins the presidency. In this election Ronald Reagan, starting (I would suppose) from the conservative box, won an overwhelming majority of conservatives and probably solid majorities of both populists and libertarians, and he won the election.

I think people will think about elections this way more as time goes on. The only problem will be when we discover that there's another important variable involved, when we will have to make the box into a cube with nine different dimensions. When we discover a fourth issue dimension, only the math whizzes will be able to understand what's going on.

Let me discuss this view of politics in two different ways: first, to take a long-range view, to try to put this four-way-matrix politics into perspective; and second, to look a little bit at the short-term prospects for change in American politics.

It seems to me that if you look at American politics over the long run—let's say going back 40 or so years, to the time of Franklin D. Roosevelt—you find that society has changed in a way that makes four-way-matrix politics more predictable, at least in retrospect.

In those 40 years, we have moved, basically, from being a nation at war to a nation at peace. As the historian William McNeill has written, war basically predisposes the nation to big government because you have to have a big government to fight a war. Because great sacrifices are being asked of people who go into combat, others feel, accordingly, that it is legitimate for government to ask for great sacrifices, like 91 percent marginal taxes. In peace, people are less disposed to accept the demands of government and less disposed to consider them legitimate.

We have also moved in these 40 years from being a country that was in depression, whose economy was considered to have a permanently high level of unemployment (people in 1945 thought we were going back to that) to a country of affluence. We've changed from being a nation that was predominantly blue collar and high-school educated or less to a country that is white collar and has a high proportion of college-educated people.

We've moved away, importantly, from being a country with a sort of cultural conformism in the fifties—a sense that it was good to be average and normal. In the fifties it was bad, in some way morally negative, to be "different," "unusual," "odd," or "eccentric." Those words were all quite negative when I was growing up. And we have become a country of very considerable cultural variety. If you could put ordinary Americans from 1949 on the streets of, not even San Francisco, but, say, Ft. Lauderdale today, they would be quite amazed at the different kinds of people they would see.

We've also moved away from a politics that basically measured people on one or two dimensions. In a mostly culturally uniform nation, we had a politics that split people on economic lines, beginning with the New Deal. (Politics had, to some extent, split people on ethnic and Civil War lines in the pre-1930 period.) So we've moved from a one-dimensional politics to a politics in which there are many cultural splits. Many different kinds of life are possible in affluent, tolerant America. And those different kinds of life, those different views of what society should do, are showing up in different clusters of issue positions that can be discerned in sizable numbers of voters.

You didn't have, 30 or 40 years ago, I suspect, nearly as many people who would have been classified under this scheme as libertarian. You had some populists, but fewer because basically people didn't divide up along these lines. Some of the issues we're talking about, many cultural issues, for example, weren't even issues in politics at that time. Economic issues were. Before about 1964, abortion wasn't an issue in American politics; it was an issue in criminal law. The only question was how to punish it, how to investigate it, and whether or not to send people to jail for it. That changed quite abruptly in the late 1960s, when it became a political issue, one of the cultural issues over which people are divided today.

So I would submit that from a long-range perspective, as we have become a culturally more various, more splintered nation, a politics that has more than two issue dimensions—that has at least four, maybe more—has developed. It makes sense to look at politics in this light.

Let me now make a few comments on what I see happening in America today to the politicians who espouse the views of the particular groups. What has happened, overall, at least in the America of early 1985, is that we have reached a kind of equilibrium on a lot of major cultural and economic issues, in the sense that people are not very eager for major change. There's not a lot of oomph behind demands for change. We've gone through a period in the 1970s when people wanted to change a great many things, when they were basically discontented with the way society worked, when they had a negative mood about society. That's very much turned around. We saw it in last year's presidential election, and we also saw how the large majority of both the Democratic congressmen and the Republican senators were reelected. It was an incumbents' year across the board, and that has consequences for all the groups we're talking about here.

First of all, the liberals have a fairly basic problem right now: no substantial bloc of voters wants a substantially larger role for government in the economy. Demands for guaranteed national income or for national health insurance are not being articulated by the politicians and do not exist in the hearts and minds of the voters. It's not something they really care about, and that poses a problem for liberal politicians in the Democratic party. The forms of increased government intervention they have sought in the past are clearly not in demand in the political market.

As for the populists, the problem is that you tend to get either incompetent or demagogic leaders espousing some of their views. It's a large constituency, but when your leadership is George Wallace or big-city, old-time hack politicians, you're not going to capture the presidency. In this day and age you're not even going to be a major factor in Congress or in most state and local governments. It's going to be difficult to have staying power. Most of the articulate opinion, whether it's liberal, conservative, or libertarian, will be arrayed against you. The populists, as they reach the point of actually having political power, tend to find the other three political groups reacting fairly strongly against them.

Conservatives face a mirror image of the liberals' problem, which is that no one really wants a substantially smaller government than we have at present, or at least there's no major constituency for that. Yes, people want things trimmed here and there and modulated and deregulated a little. But once you start talking about proposals to cut Social Security and student loans, you suddenly find yourself beset by great beehives of protest. The political system reacts with great speed, and those proposals are deep-sixed pretty rapidly.

What about the libertarians? I see some problems here as well. Some of the people this morning may have presented a more hopeful scenario for political libertarians than I would suggest exists. The baby-boom generation has rightly been portrayed as generally having less interventionist views on economic questions because it's basically an affluent generation, and a more libertarian view on cultural issues because it's a culturally liberated generation. It really doesn't want to be bothered with restrictions. However, the baby-boom generation, if defined as people born between 1947 and 1962, peaked as a percentage of the electorate in 1984. There won't be much change in that proportion over the next 10 or 12 years. But we are not working up toward some Everest-like peak of baby-boom participation in the future. What you see is what you got.

In considering some of the issues that have become important in the last year, it seems to me that the country has moved a little bit away from a libertarian direction. And I would suggest two ways that has happened. First, I sense a rise in nationalism, an almost aggressive foreign policy feeling. From Reagan's participation in the Normandy ceremony, which was featured very movingly in his campaign film, to the Olympics, which was stage-managed by *Time's* Man of the Year, who was Michael Deaver's college roommate, you get a communitarian rather than libertarian view with nationalism. I sense a kind of fellow feeling that in some ways is analogous to the spirit of a war situation.

Second, I sense a moralistic backlash against some of the libertarian trends of behavior in the last 20 years. As the baby boomers grow older, as they start acting more like parents than like teenagers, they will react somewhat against some of the ideas they used to think were so terrific. Take the abortion issue. Justice Blackmun's decision in *Roe* v. *Wade*, written in 1972 but announced in 1973 so it could be delayed until after Nixon's reinauguration, talks about abortion as a marvelous thing that's going to solve all of society's problems. It's going to get rid of air pollution and water pollution, end the evils of overpopulation and the overuse of resources by affluent countries, safeguard personal freedom—everything is going to be solved. You don't hear that kind of rhapsodic view of abortion today, even among abortion-rights supporters, among whom I guess I would number myself. Abortion is basically viewed with distaste—as something unpleasant but sadly necessary—or as something that people ought to have the option of doing. That's a different attitude.

Abortion opponents have had some success in the battle of ideas, some of it based on the underlying communitarian assumption that we have duties toward the unborn and that there are certain things a community shouldn't allow to happen even if individuals want it to happen. This feeling has a tendency to undermine the libertarian point of view.

Both this nationalism and this moralism are only, at most, trends in one direction. They're not necessarily sweeping the country, and they're not affecting everybody in each of the four categories in the same ways. But they are trends.

And that suggests some problems. In the short run, at least, in a country where we have a political equilibrium and no blazing discontent with the way things are, I have difficulty seeing where any of these groups is going to make any headway.

Terry Nichols Clark: I will offer an interpretation consistent with comments here by some other speakers, but which goes beyond them by placing changes in political views within a broader analytical framework.

Let me lead off by briefly locating my comments in context. The interpretation I will summarize was developed in the late 1970s as part of the Fiscal Strain Project at the University of Chicago and National Opinion Research Center. The project included some 25 students and research associates working together for seven years. We were convinced by about 1976 that major changes were underway in American political culture and set out to analyze them systematically. NORC is known for its citizen surveys, but we also wanted good information about leaders since they articulate changes more clearly than most citizens. We thus subscribed to newspapers from cities as diverse as Boston and San Diego, interviewed numerous public officials, completed case studies of unusual leaders and cities, and conducted and analyzed national sample surveys of mayors and council members as well as citizens. The results have appeared in several places, but the main report is *City Money* (Columbia University Press, 1983), which Lorna Ferguson and I coauthored.

The taxpayers' revolt provides a critical test for competing interpretations of politics. It did not begin nationally, in 1980, with the election of Ronald Reagan and the Republican capture of the Senate. Nor did it begin at the state level, as has been widely stated, in 1978, with Proposition 13 in California or Proposition 2½ in Massachusetts. It began locally, in 1974, when half of American cities began cutting back or slowing their growth of expenditures. This was not recognized nationally at the time. It's only becoming clear now, as documented in our book *City Money*. It was a true sea change because of its critical turning-around of the growth of government.

It began quietly with the election of new city council members and mayors. It was not publicized in referenda or in a visibly discussed national election. The lesson I draw is that it's important to look at what's happening locally for a clearer view of sharp alternatives than at presidential candidates who are all looking for the middle. Localities, smaller and more homogeneous in their constituencies, permit formulating alternative policies in a clearer way and implementing citizen preferences more conspicuously than do heterogeneous constituencies—bigger cities, states, the national society. Consequently, citizen preferences are more directly expressed in policy than are preferences of special-interest groups, which are more powerful at the state and national levels.

Since the decline of the parties in the early 1970s, many of our political dynamics, nationally as well as locally, have involved battles between citizens, on the one hand, and organized groups, on the other. You have theories emphasizing each: Anthony Downs's economic theory of democracy, stressing citizen preferences; and the group theory approach, the mainstream political science tradition from Arthur Bentley, V. O. Key, Robert Dahl, and others. Both theories, I suggest, are partially correct in that they identify elements that may be important, but only for particular contexts, not all the time.

Where and how? This is what we address in *City Money*, a table from which is presented here. It illustrates the complexities that Michael Barone said might be impossible to understand without higher math. Yet it's really not that difficult. We have five dimensions across the top instead of just two. Down the left side of the table we have four types of political culture, very similar to those of Maddox and Lilie. Our labels are a bit different, but basically we're generating the same four boxes that they discuss because the

Table 1
FOUR LOCAL POLITICAL CULTURES

Political Culture	Policy Preferences		Sources of Public Input		Policy Strategies
	Fiscal Liberalism	Social Liberalism	Individual Citizen	Organized Group	
Democrats (e.g., Boston)	✔	✔		✔	Find new revenue
Republicans (e.g., San Diego)			✔		Across-the-board budget cuts
Ethnics (e.g., Gary, Ind.)	✔			✔	Similar to Democrats
New Fiscal Populists (e.g., Houston)		✔	✔		Improve productivity

basic dimensions are still fiscal and social liberalism. You could relabel their four-fold box the same as ours. What we add are the three other dimensions to the right and an analysis of why these elements hold together.

This way of analyzing both individual citizens and organized groups using the dimensions of fiscal and social liberalism is a way of reconciling ostensibly contradictory theories by pointing out the conditions under which one or the other is more important. Individual citizens are less important in the political cultures of cities and national societies dominated by traditional Democrats and ethnic politicians, who listen more to the constituencies of the New Deal coalition—the party, the union, the church, the ethnic group as an organized entity. By contrast, the individual citizen is more visible and legitimate for traditional Republicans and the new fiscal populists, or "libertarians" in Maddox and Lilie's terms.

Let me say a few words about our five basic dimensions, the "deep structures" from which different political structures are generated. There has indeed been a relative increase in fiscal conservatism over time, as we've seen in 20 years of surveys by the National Opinion Research Center and other organizations.

Now consider the second dimension, social liberalism. This label is interesting and important, and I would very much underscore the comments of Lee Atwater and Michael Barone that we should not overgeneralize. American citizens are not supporting radical-chic, late-sixties lifestyles. Most Americans are much closer to the center, and when we talk about "social liberalism" or "social tolerance," we mean extending to a communist the right to speak—extending the right to talk about these issues in a general forum. On these social and civil-liberties issues the American citizenry continues to move in a socially tolerant direction, even over the 1970s and 1980s, when some have talked about a backlash or a New Right.

The third dimension of political culture is the emphasis on individual citizens as legitimate policymakers, and the fourth is the emphasis on organized groups as legitimate policymakers. The fifth dimension concerns specific policies that flow from the other dimensions. These five dimensions are the deep structures of all political systems. They combine variously in different contexts, cities, and time periods to generate new alternatives and possible combinations. We focus on four of these political cultures, listed down the side of Table 1. The first three—traditional Democrats, traditional Republicans, and ethnic politicians—were found from the 1930s up to the 1970s. The fourth type emerged only in the 1970s in sufficient numbers to be measured. This type is our new fiscal populists, or the libertarians of Maddox and Lilie. The important and interesting difference is that the new fiscal populists are socially liberal and socially tolerant at the same time that they are fiscally conservative. But beyond that, we stress their political dynamics, how they emerge and act as leaders.

Here I disagree with Bill Schneider's comment that all Americans are populist. Rather, the populist style is one that politicians stress when they are on the outs. Unable to get themselves nominated through their party by espousing the dominant ideology, they have to attack the party by appealing to individual citizens. If they cannot get campaign funds from unions, party organizers, and the establishment, then they appeal to average Joes.

New fiscal populists have difficult careers. They have often lost nominations and had to run as independents. They have had to fight their way up, and thus they have been more successful locally, where parties are weak. They've had an especially hard time becoming presidential or national candidates.

Thus you have a major conflict between an orientation to citizens, on the one hand, and an orientation to organized groups, on the other. In this regard, new fiscal populists are the Weberian carriers of citizen preferences. Their enemies are municipal employee unions, traditional Democrats, and others who oppose policies the fiscal populists seek to implement. One of their most important policies is improving government productivity, which is the only way to reduce taxes—or at least hold taxes down—and yet simultaneously to be socially liberal, in the sense of responding to the disadvantaged. You can provide services to the disadvantaged and hold down taxes only if you make government more efficient.

The new fiscal populists are the most critical political type that emerged from our citizen-survey trends and our analyses of local officials in *City Money*. They carry the flame of the taxpayers' revolt, along with traditional Republicans, who were too small in number to win alone. Howard Jarvis had placed tax reform referenda on the California ballot for years, but they never passed until lots of people with Democratic backgrounds supported him. This development of fiscally conservative Democrats was important not only in California, as people initially suggested, but nationally.

The dynamics of the new fiscal populists are clearer when you look at some mayors. It was in talking with these local officials that we became persuaded of how important this new political movement was as early as 1976 or 1977.

Peter Flaherty in Pittsburgh was one of the first fiscal populist mayors. He was elected in 1969 after running as an independent Democrat against the Democratic organization and against the Republicans. Once in office, he fought the major organization within the city council, the Teamsters Union. They took him on for saying that he wanted to change the rule requiring water-meter installers in Pittsburgh to have drivers, or "chauffeurs," as they were designated by the media. When the Teamsters called a city-wide strike, the average steel worker backed the mayor against the union. It was a perfect populist issue. It permitted Flaherty to establish his legitimacy with the average citizen and to be reelected four years later, despite the bitter opposition of the municipal employee unions, the press, the business elite, the civic elite, and most other organized groups.

Flaherty was a populist who appealed to the broad, unorganized middle class, as have certain other leaders in other cities. Edward Koch in New York was the least known of the candidates. Bill Green in Philadelphia, Kathy Whitmire in Houston, Dianne Feinstein in San Francisco—all are new fiscal populists, albeit Koch more in his campaign than in office. They combine their fiscal conservatism with a social liberalism, opposing organized groups and instead appealing to citizens as a means of implementing and legitimizing their policies.

One important point that has been made in this conference is connecting the baby boom with the political ideological configuration. That is, you want to look not just at the four-fold typology, but at which of the four cells are growing or declining, and why. And that's a critical element, one that has been missed in many earlier, similar-looking analyses. The same four-fold typology was used by Seymour Martin Lipset, Bill Schneider, and others 10 or 15 years ago, but they didn't draw the same conclusions that we have.

The major concept they used was the "new class." Irving Kristol and Aaron Wildavsky used it, and Nathan Glazer and others talked about it. In the late sixties and early seventies, the youth generation was called a "new class," which was, in terms of the four-fold typology, clearly liberal on social issues, in favor of personal tolerance, civil liberties, and the like. But this class was also seen as supporting expansive government. Growth of government was very much a part of the late sixties and early seventies generation, and what we're talking about today is a major shift.

Those who held the view that the new class was the expansive social force in America saw that fourth box of "fiscally conservative, socially liberal," as a small group. They were wrong. In that sense, the box was also identified by Lipset, Everett Ladd, and others as a small, exclusively Republican sort of cell. Also, I think Pat Caddell must have misremembered the Warren Miller book he mentioned because it too really took the same position as Lipset and Ladd in seeing the "new class" as the right interpretation of the baby boom rather than this new fiscal populist or libertarian position.

The discussion this morning also brought out the fact that there are very few ethnic politicians or new fiscal populists represented in national policy, in the House of Representatives or the Senate. Indeed, it is at the local level that you can find these because the parties are so powerful at the state and federal levels.

I would thus qualify the importance of special-interest groups and the inability of the individual to rise without the support of a party. The populist style of the new fiscal populist leaders is likely to continue as long as the parties remain frozen in the traditional New Deal Democrat or New Deal Republican positions. The more the parties open up, the less it will be necessary for individuals to appeal in populist style to citizens for legitimacy, and the more individuals can act with the support of the organized party or group.

Let me conclude by mentioning what the new fiscal populists have implemented as actual policies. Since policy choices are often more sharply defined at the local level, one way of considering alternative policies nationally is to look at how they've actually been implemented locally. We've been studying three basic kinds of policies—expenditure reduction, revenue raising, and increasing productivity. The new fiscal populists were most clearly pursuing those that increased productivity. The ethnic politicians were doing the opposite.

We're monitoring this now with the most extensive study of local government ever undertaken. I'm coordinating 26 teams of policy analysts who are surveying every U.S. city of over 25,000. It's called the Fiscal Austerity and Urban Innovation Project. We received sufficient data a few months ago to produce a paper on 427 cities, and the same basic methodology is being used in 25 other countries. Many similar developments are taking place even in Western Europe, where there's a breakdown of traditional left and right. It is illuminating indeed to look at how this is taking place internationally.

Question: *It seems to me that the civil rights movement of the sixties is a basic component of what made the baby boomers the baby boomers. It doesn't seem clear to me, especially from Mr. Maddox and Mr. Lilie's comments, how that is accounted for in your typology. Certainly it's government intervention, but at the same time it's tolerance. So how do you fit it in?*

Maddox: We don't. If you look at survey questions through the fifties, sixties, and the seventies, you find that what was a fairly divisive set of issues in the fifties becomes almost consensual in the sixties. That is, if you asked people in the mid-sixties whether the federal government should pursue desegregation, you got overwhelmingly positive responses. Then, by the late sixties and early seventies, when you got into specifics, such as busing, there was a flip-flop—a lot of opposition, but again almost a kind of consensual response. So the four categories that we use don't separate people according to civil rights opinions precisely because the responses tend to be so consensual. What opposition to civil rights you could glean from those survey results would probably come from the populists, but that's speculation.

Lilie: There's also, I might add, a philosophical problem that you've raised. If, in general, you think of high levels of personal freedom as meaning nonintervention, how do you approach those issues in which government intervention is proposed as a way of increasing personal freedoms—civil rights in the fifties and sixties, and perhaps affirmative action in the sixties and seventies? This is a tricky question, and it's not clear what the liberal position, the libertarian position, and so on, would be. So we've tended to try to stay away from this kind of question in making up the categories.

Clark: It's useful in terms of understanding those two dimensions to break up civil rights into two parts: support for government, and support for racial and ethnic equality. In that sense the classic questions are, "Would you invite a black to your home for dinner?" and "Would you let your daughter marry a black?" and so forth. There is an increasing tolerance on such questions over time, whereas policies involving the active involvement of government—busing is the clearest example—show the opposite. So Americans have grown increasingly tolerant on a social level at the same time that they're resistant to the use of powerful government.

Question: *Mr. Lilie and Mr. Maddox talked about the four different groups in the context of 1988 and how the fight for the presidential nomination would go in each party. What's really relevant in fighting for a party's nomination is the party activists. Do you know, in each of the two parties, where the party activists fall in each of these categories?*

Maddox: No, we don't have any surveys that look specifically at party activists. The data we have from nationwide surveys are not broken down according to activists because the numbers would be so small that the results would be very unreliable. We would need to conduct a nationwide survey directed specifically at party activists on both sides.

Clark: We've addressed this question with mayors and council members because they are more active than citizens. We've often asked them, "Where do you agree or disagree with your citizens on these issues?" Compared with citizens, they more consistently fall into the classic New Deal Democrat and New Deal Republican boxes, and there will be far fewer of them in the off-diagonals. They'll say, "I'm a Democrat; I want to spend more than my citizens," or "I'm a Republican; I want to spend less," and so forth. Citizens are more frequently new fiscal populists.

Barone: One thing to remember is that the groups of party activists—people sufficiently active to participate in a caucus, or the broader group that votes in a party primary—are like accordions: they can get bigger or smaller as they include or disinclude certain people. We've got a pretty good sense of who were the party activists in each of the parties in 1976, 1980, and 1984. The Republican group in the last several elections has tended to be disproportionately conservative in comparison with the party followers. The Democratic activists have definitely been disproportionately liberal, with maybe a few more libertarians and a few less populists than the typical group of party voters.

Sometimes that is the result of accidents of character in the candidates. For example, the candidacies of the Democratic candidates in 1984 who were less liberal on economic issues collapsed for reasons that didn't have a lot to do with issues. This was particularly true in the case of John Glenn; he had to face a Democratic primary electorate that was biased toward the liberal side. And if you look at turnout in a lot of Southern states, many people who used to vote in Democratic primaries seemed to say, "None of these candidates is for me; I'm not in the picture anymore." So the Democratic convention reflected that group of liberals more than it would have if Glenn had been a viable candidate, which, I submit, his issue positions didn't prevent him from being.

Thomas Moore, *Fortune:* *I'm curious about the level of intensity that the various categories measure. To what extent does the diversification of categories merely reflect people turning off to politics altogether?*

Maddox: The questions that were used to measure the two dimensions don't really tap intensity, but one piece of evidence that gives you an idea of how much intensity the groups attach to their views is voter turnout. The populists are the category least likely to turn out. In fact, the majority of them don't even get to the voting booth. So populism in some respects has much less in the way of intense supporters. The two categories with the highest turnouts throughout the 1970s and up through 1980 were the libertarians and the conservatives. That's a pretty good explanation of a Ronald Reagan victory; those people not only supported him but turned out at very high rates. Liberals, interestingly enough—and this says a little bit about the state of the Democratic party, I guess—were fairly intense in turning out to vote in the early seventies but have fallen off since then.

Clark: Yours is a critical question that has misled many elected officials as well as pollsters, especially on fiscal issues. Most pollsters in the 1970s asked, "Would you like to see your city (or your national government) do more or less of the same in the following areas: police, fire, sewage, education, welfare, and so forth?" Most people said they wanted more. Most people want more services if you don't impose a budget constraint. That was why many persons claimed, right after Proposition 13, that most Americans still want more government. But ask Americans—or anybody else in the world—if they want to pay more taxes, and everyone will say no. So the question is, how do we harmonize the answers to "Do you want to pay more taxes?" and "Do you want more services from your government?"

Most survey items have not included a way of doing that. We did so by analyzing the question, "What's the most important problem facing America today?" Throughout the mid- to late sixties, it was race and foreign relations, mainly Vietnam. That changed drastically in 1972–73, when such problems as the oil crisis and inflation gained visibility over race and social issues. Much more importantly, 60–70 percent of Americans replied that the most important problems were economic issues: taxes, inflation, and the like. Many persons—Marty Lipset, Bill Schneider, and others—have published papers arguing that Americans have not grown more fiscally conservative. They are right in the limited sense that Americans continued to give a liberal answer to such questions as "Do you want more government spending?" But they're wrong in the sense that the importance of those issues has diminished compared with the importance of the answer to "How much are you willing to pay in taxes?" Witness, if you will, not just turnout in elections but the drastic tax-reduction referenda, which are inconsistent with surveys saying that citizens want more government spending. They want the services. But when push comes to shove, many citizens have said, "I'll take lower taxes and Ronald Reagan if he can accomplish that better." Fiscal issues are now more important to many Americans than government-service issues.

V. Ideas in American Politics

Paul H. Weaver: There are times when I think that the subject of ideas in politics may be the most hateful thing imaginable. Good ideas clarify, but bad ideas conceal and mislead. It often seems to me, as I think about modern ideas and modern-day politics, that most of the ideas that prevail today are of the concealing and misleading sort. In fact, I think it's fair to say that our society—particularly its most ideological and articulate elements—is positively awash in false consciousness. We can see this most clearly among political intellectuals.

First, on the left we have the liberal intellectuals, who in their ideological pronouncements express great sympathy for the poor, sympathy for the redistribution of wealth, and concern for the plight of suffering victims. But in their own personal lives they live very well indeed, often very upscale, and support government programs that, rhetoric aside, actually redistribute power and wealth from the lower to the upper echelons of society. In short, on the left we find the principle, "Think left, live right."

We find a very comparable situation among our conservative and neoconservative intellectuals, but it's reversed. These are people who write books and give lectures on such topics as the "defense of the bourgeois family," the "importance of traditional values," and the "necessity of religion as a force in democratic and civilized society." When you look at their private lives and personal attitudes and behavior, however, these are highly modernist people indeed. They may believe in the traditional family, but they practice women's liberation and all the other modes of modern liberation. Intellectual defenders of religion, they are themselves nonbelievers and nonpractitioners; many neoconservative intellectuals define themselves as "nonobservant Orthodox Jews," whatever that might mean.

It is not only among intellectuals that false consciousness of this sort is a problem. Something very comparable also afflicts our most basic pictures of society and political economy. Let me describe one element of this basic mythology about our society, explain a few ways in which I think it's inadequate, and suggest how it has come to pass that society is at a very interesting, if unrecognized, turning point both politically and intellectually.

Let me begin with the mythology. This is the familiar notion that our society is basically a free-enterprise society and that, in particular, our political economy is based on the notion of limited government, free markets, and free exchange; that this political system is supported most strongly by business and by forces that we think of as "conservative"; and that these forces are facing off against another set of forces: liberals and organized labor. This second set is more or less collectivist, believes in government intervention, and is no great defender of markets or the classical liberal idea of individual rights and freedoms. Popular wisdom has it that our politics and national political/cultural life consist very much of the struggle between these two forces and ideas.

Now, the fact is that this picture is almost completely false. The truth about American political economy, at least for the last century or so, is that far from having been based on the idea of free markets, it has been based much more clearly and consistently on the idea of managed markets—on the idea that government correctly intervenes in the economy to manage its course, to limit entry, to do all kinds of things to determine economic outcomes. This is an idea, moreover, that has been supported almost universally throughout all sectors of our society. It's been supported—and this is something we do understand and recognize instinctively—by many forces of the left. But it has been supported equally by business.

One can look back in business history, as I did this year while writing a book about business politics, and ask, What did business say and think back in the Golden Age when business is supposed to have supported the free market and embodied a kind of unapologetic capitalist view of the world? Well, you read back and you read back and you never find the Golden Age because it never existed. American business has always favored government management of markets. This was most clearly embodied in business support for tariffs throughout the nineteenth century and well into the twentieth century, as we are all aware. But we're not so clearly aware of just how important business support for tariffs was and what it meant intellectually and politically for business to do this—systematically and across the board, as it did.

The truth is that the ideology of American business for at least a century has been corporatism—government management of the economy. And the ideology of American management has been managerialism—the domination of professional managers who serve all the different corporate interest groups: shareholders, labor, the local community, and customers. Of course, in the end managers always benefited themselves most clearly and consistently. That has been the reality of the politics of American business. Overlaid upon it has been the populist myth—but it's also a business-supported myth—of the free-enterprise economy supported by business and opposed by the left.

It is also interesting that as the twentieth century wore on, at least for the first half of the century, this corporatist and managerialist ideology became more powerful in our society. You find it sweeping the agricultural community at the turn of the century as the farm movement gave up on the idea of free markets and opposition to tariffs and embraced the notion, first, of farmers' cooperatives, and then of government intervention in and management of farm production, farm entry, farm pricing, farm everything. Thus in the 1920s and 1930s, agriculture became a more clearly procorporatist, pro-managerialist sector than it had been before.

In the 1920s you find an extraordinary and little-understood movement throughout society for occupational licensure. After World War I there was a movement, primarily at the state and local levels, for government to manage entry into and conduct in businesses of the most innocent sort, like cutting hair and driving taxicabs and all kinds of things for which market mechanisms work perfectly well—except that Americans didn't believe in market mechanisms. Everyone was caught up in the notion that things go better if markets are managed by government.

Then, in the 1930s the Democratic party was captured by this idea in the form of the New Deal. Throughout this period, business was an active advocate of government economic planning. The main ideological and political impetus behind the first NRA proposals that FDR handed down came from big business—from the heads of General Electric and U.S. Steel, from the leaders of the biggest institutions of American capitalism because they believed in the management of the economy. All of this culminated in the rise of the labor unions to real power in the thirties and forties and, of course, with government management of our society during World War II.

Since the war, this corporatist regime has weakened continually in every sphere—institutional, ideological, intellectual, cultural.

This collapse, which, again, I think we don't recognize very clearly, is best symbolized by two contrasting events in the history of the economics profession.

In 1929 Irving Fisher, the great professor of economics at Yale, conducted a little survey of the American Economic Association's membership, asking them to send him their personal economic assessments of the economic rationality and justification of Prohibition—the laws against the sale and consumption of alcoholic beverages. Fisher summed up the reports of his members in his presidential address to the association: every economist who responded in the survey had stated that, in his own personal belief, there were net economic benefits from Prohibition, that, on balance, Prohibition was a good thing. It made American workers work harder, it meant that they didn't waste their hard-won resources on something silly and destructive, it made absenteeism lower, and on and on and on. These economists were full of appreciation for the benefits of what we, today, would consider absolutely an outrageous intervention by government into a matter that's essentially private. The economics profession back then believed in corporatist economics. It did not believe in free-market individual choice.

Two generations later, in the late 1960s and early 1970s, the Brookings Institution—although originally an institution created by a business leader and embodying business ideas of public policy but later transformed into what's conventionally seen as a liberal political institution—began to convene conferences and commission books by economists on government regulation. Of course, the regulatory programs that attracted the most attention at the time were those that had been set up in the 1930s: the cartel-like structures created for regulating the transportation, communications, and other industries. By the late 1960s, when Brookings sought competent, professionally accredited economists to study the net social costs and benefits of regulatory programs of this sort, they couldn't find any economists who would argue that, on balance, these programs were beneficial. Suddenly, opinion among liberal economists took a fascinating tip at the end of the sixties, shifting sharply and decisively in favor of markets in an ever-widening array of situations.

Let me now just name a few of the forces that have led to the crumbling of corporatist and managerialist America.

First, and very important but little recognized, is the rise in the market for corporate control—the absolutely crucial increase in the frequency and success of hostile takeover bids in the stock market. Until the 1960s the hostile takeover bid was a rarity; it almost never occurred. Managers of big American corporations could be pretty well assured that their companies wouldn't be taken over and that there was no real, serious threat to their domination of their companies through the stock market, that is, from the shareholder. Today that is obviously no longer true. No company is too big to be taken over, and corporation managers know that the lower the company's stock—and thus the poorer the management is performing—the more likely a takeover is. This has been a terrific spur to the management of American economic institutions, and believe me, company managers are behaving differently and performing better today than they were 10 years ago.

A second force is the entry of America into the global economy, which is also a thing of the last two decades, and the rise in this global economy of huge institutions perfectly competitive with our own—the Japanese automobile and steel companies, of course, but really companies around the world. American companies can no longer be assured, as they once were, that government intervention isn't much of a risk to them, that it will only benefit them by curbing competition. Today a government regulation may saddle an American company with a cost or a risk that a foreign competitor doesn't have, and the foreign competitor may clean up on this. This is a big change, and it's leading to significant changes in the politics of American business.

Another very important factor is the deregulation of the labor markets in the United States, the receding presence of labor unions, and the weakening power of unions to determine wage levels.

A fourth phenomenon is the rise of a new class. Among people who are professional and college educated, there is a growing insistence on basing personal beliefs and actions on personal choice and rejecting traditional forms of received authority, on personal lifestyle values, on religious belief, and so on. The rise of this new class ethos of cultural individualism is important to our political culture. It makes people much less deferential to institutions of all kinds and much more insistent on their own individual authority in politics, in markets, in everything. It is eroding every institution of corporatist America.

Finally—and this won't sound nice—I would point to the rise, spread, and perfection of the art of public relations. One of the principal inventions of the managerial corporation in the twentieth century has been PR—invented discourse for the purpose of manipulating appearances, moving public opinion, justifying actions or situations that are desired for some other reason. Public relations is practiced universally by managers of all American institutions—not just in business, but in government, politics, labor, universities, and journalism. People who see PR practiced up close can respond to it only in one of two possible ways. Either they accept it and thus deny what they are witnessing, which is a kind of systematic lying about what companies and people really think and perceive, or they experience a revulsion against it. The fact is, and this is borne out amply by public opinion polls, the overwhelming majority of people react negatively. They don't deny it; they admit what they are experiencing, which is a lot of official institutional lying, and they don't like it. That, I believe, is the underlying experience that explains the incredible decline of American institutions' standing in public esteem. Across the board, from business to medicine to labor to politics to Congress to bureaucracy, the standing of institutions in public opinion polls has decreased dramatically over the past two decades.

We no longer respect the institutions, such as government institutions, that managed the economy and presided over a corporatist, managerialist America. The result is a crumbling of this old, managed, political economy. And what is coming in its place? Well, that's the big issue, and I think it's impossible to say for sure, but I don't think there's much doubt that corporatist America is dying and that it's not going to be revived. Its basis in our moral imagination, in our economic experiences, in our institutions, has simply crumbled.

It seems to me that we are now rushing off in two quite different directions. On the one hand, we see the failures of institutions and tell ourselves that we've got to intervene and reform them; so, one public response to the crumbling of corporate America is to try to rebuild big government. But that never works. It's a vicious cycle, and it only damages the institutions and weakens government's own standing in the public esteem.

On the other hand, another kind of public reaction is gaining momentum, and that is, first, a simple withdrawal of faith from all institutions, across the board (which we've seen), and second, a kind of slow voting with one's feet in terms of occupation, beliefs, life-style, you name it—a withdrawing of consent for policies and career lines and everything associated with corporatist America.

That is why young union members vote for Ronald Reagan. That is why the culture heroes of our time are not the Lee Iacoccas but the entrepreneurs. And the only thing that might appeal to us about Lee Iacocca is that his career does embody a kind of entrepreneurial rags-to-riches theme even though he's a corporatist and a managerialist through and through. This voting with the feet is even embodied in our rock music lyrics and ethos, which is absolutely a celebration of freedom.

So this is where we are: at a moment when the old order is crumbling but with ideas so unclear, fitting so badly the reality of what used to be and what has happened, that we cannot understand the extraordinary opportunity and turning point that we have reached. And the question, of course, is, what will we turn to next? My own feeling is that it's more or less inevitable that we will drift toward a kind of "proto-neolibertarianism." (I apologize for the phrase.) By this, I do not mean that we're going to see anarchism or a withering of the state. I do mean that we're going to see, as we have seen already, a real change in the moral and political sympathies of the American people: Americans will come to believe in paternalism even less, and in the authority of the individual to control his own life even more.

Beyond that, I don't know what will happen. But the shift from corporatism to individualism is a big, big change in the broad outlines of our society and our world. I think it's a good one. I welcome it. I like it. I think it makes this a fascinating time to live in.

As a final word, I would note that the conflict between these two ideas, individualism and corporatism, is perhaps most sharply defined within the Reagan administration, within the camp that conventionally—though I think often wrongly—is defined as conservatism. Within the Reagan administration, within Reagan himself, there can be found two warring ideas. I think of them as, on the one hand, the free-market idea, and on the other, "Deaverism." But that may not be fair. So let me say, the free-market idea vs. the idea of managerialism and corporatism, that is, the old interest-group corporatist world. The president embodies both ideas passionately, and he rattles back and forth between them. We have an administration and a president that you can imagine withdrawing from NATO, or being "super-Carterist" in foreign policy, or being absolutely hawkish and warlike—anything is possible. What happens to Reagan, what happens after Reagan, will be a big part of the story.

Edward H. Crane: When David Boaz suggested I speak at this conference for 15 minutes on the subject of ideas in American politics, I asked, "Isn't that a bit long?" I'm rarely at a loss for words, but talking for 15 minutes on what passes for ideas in American politics is, well, something of a challenge. There is, unfortunately, not a lot to talk about.

I say "unfortunately" because I believe the freedoms and prosperity we enjoy as a nation today are due primarily to what was actually quite an avid interest in political ideas on the part of the vast majority of intelligent Americans during the period immediately preceding and following the American Revolution. Ours is perhaps a unique heritage in modern times, this tradition of the active involvement of the intelligent lay public in the debate over the issues of the day. And of course, the revolutionary period benefited from the ideas of some of the greatest political thinkers of any period—like Thomas Paine, George Mason, Samuel Adams, and Thomas Jefferson.

According to historian Bernard Bailyn, there were some 1,500 political pamphlets published during the 20-year revolutionary period, mostly by ordinary Americans. "They did not transcend the ordinary limitations of their trade," Bailyn wrote. "They were rarely principals in the controversies of the time. The American pamphleteers were almost to a man lawyers, ministers, merchants, or planters heavily engaged in their occupations." The American writers, he said, were "profoundly reasonable people . . . who sought to convince their opponents rather than annihilate them."

Thomas Paine's brilliant little booklet *Common Sense* was read by just about every literate person in the colonies. More than 120,000 copies were printed in a population of about 3 million. That is equivalent to about 9 million copies today, when a book is considered a best seller if it hits five digits.

Out of all this intellectual ferment and mass participation in political debate, of course, emerged a nation based on individual rights to life, liberty, and property that was, quite literally, the envy of the world. And as I mentioned, we continue to benefit from the political system they established more than 200 years ago.

But it seems to me that our political system is increasingly being transformed into something quite different from what the Founders intended, into a system that tolerates a far greater level of intervention on behalf of the state, both domestically and internationally, than was ever contemplated by those remarkable people who established this nation. I would further argue that this transformation has occurred in concert with a steady and significant decline in the percentage of intelligent Americans who participate in or even care about political debate.

Indeed, the level of political debate in America has sunk so low as to be virtually devoid of ideas. Political campaigns are run on the basis of images, personalities, and slogans. Ideas are strictly verboten. You can almost hear the campaign manager cackle with glee when an opposing candidate slips up and injects an idea into the campaign. He knows the media will play up the conflict and opposition the idea is sure to generate. Imagine a man of Thomas Jefferson's intellectual integrity facing a rejoinder from a grinning Walter Mondale, "Where's the beef, Tom?" Or imagine Jefferson or Mason confronted with Ronald Reagan running a presidential campaign featuring a patriotic country-and-western song and a "We're number one" pitch, perhaps more appropriate to a Redskins' football advertising campaign.

Presidential campaigns in this country, for as far back as one might care to recall, have been distinguished by their utter lack of ideological content, not to mention substantive ideas. One side wants a "compassionate" America, the other a "strong" America. Neither side is particularly interested in spelling out the policy implications of their slogans. Certainly neither side is about to challenge the status quo with respect to any significant federal program.

The American public, for its part, seems increasingly bored by presidential campaigns—and who can really blame them? But the questions before us are, why has the public become so disinterested in political campaigns and political philosophy? Why have campaigns become so devoid of intellectual content? And, then, what can be done about it?

Let me offer several possible answers. First, the twentieth century has seen the rise of "experts" in the social sciences: Ph.D.'s whose arguments from authority are designed to shut off dissent and encourage the "non-expert" to keep his mouth shut. So-and-so has a Ph.D., you know, and so who are you to question what he's proposing? Since many of these so-called experts end up as court intellectuals, what they often are proposing is a defense of the status quo and an expansion of existing programs.

I would also argue that the expansion and centralization of the public school monopoly has had a chilling impact on intellectual curiosity in America. This shows up in test scores that are much lower today than they were two decades ago. It is also inevitable in a system in which a state board of education presumes to approve, say, two or three civics textbooks—none significantly different from the others—for consumption by hundreds of thousands of students. Where is the competition of ideas in such a system? How does such a system stimulate intellectual curiosity with its homogenized product? What can we expect other than the academic mediocrity we see each year coming out of our public high schools—schools protected from competition and, hence, cut off from the possibility of innovation and intellectual stimulation?

There are other, more immediate, causes for this decline of public interest in political ideas. One that deserves mention is the Federal Election Campaign Act. It seems strange that this act was passed in response to the abuses of Watergate. If Watergate proved anything, it is that Lord Acton was right about power corrupting. So what does Congress do to remedy the situation? It increases the power of the federal government. The problem, it seems to me, is not with the milk lobby bribing politicians, but rather with politicians having the power to hand price supports to the dairy industry. But that's a digression. The point is, the FECA has had a stifling impact—and a predictably stifling impact, I might add—on political debate in America. The $1,000 limit on contributions to federal campaigns has not only discouraged individuals from participating in campaigns, it has greatly reduced the ability of non-established candidates to make themselves heard. And these are precisely the candidates most likely to have new ideas. The contribution limitation is analogous to Sears passing a law saying, "Anyone can compete with us, but only up to $1,000 in advertising." A new idea, a new approach that a non-established candidate might bring forth needs large amounts of seed capital, just as a new product does. It's obvious, for instance, that Gene McCarthy could never have galvanized the anti-Vietnam War sentiment in America and effectively forced Lyndon Johnson out of the 1968 presidential campaign had the FECA been in force back then.

Let me also suggest that the media themselves are responsible for the decline in interest in political ideas. The national media, with notable exceptions such as Bill Moyers and Ted Koppel, are transfixed by the idea of a campaign as a horse race. The substance, the ideas that should be integral to a campaign for president are really of very little interest to most of the media. Give them a "Where's the beef?" or a shot of Gary Hart jogging, and they'll take it over a substantive issue any day.

A prime example of what I'm talking about was the 1980 campaign, when Ronald Reagan, Jimmy Carter, and most of the intelligent media knew very well that the Social Security system was on the brink of collapse. Here was the largest single program in the federal government, representing 30 percent of the federal budget, in a state of crisis. Because neither Reagan nor Carter chose to talk about it, it was completely ignored in the campaign and the American people were given no clue as to what was pending. And what was the major domestic crisis by the second year of the new Reagan administration? Social Security. If the issue had been aired during the campaign, some truly innovative approaches to solving the problem might have been tried, rather than the higher-tax, status quo approach of the Greenspan Commission.

The lack of seriousness with which much of the media treats political philosophy in general and public policy in particular is also evidenced in the media's insistence that President Reagan is a committed free-market ideologue, practically a libertarian. In fact, Ronald Reagan is a New Deal Republican. He's not kidding when he says he admires FDR more than any other president, which he's been saying at least as far back as the 1950s. When he was governor of California, state taxes and state spending increased in real terms per capita faster than at any time in the state's history—before or after. Compared with Ronald Reagan, Jerry Brown was a fiscal conservative. A responsible media would look beyond President Reagan's compelling free-market rhetoric, consider the record, and report on the reality.

A most revealing event that illustrates Ronald Reagan's true ideological orientation is described by Lou Cannon in his excellent book *Reagan*. In his book Cannon describes the process by which Governor Reagan went about selecting a replacement for Lt. Gov. Bob Finch, who had been chosen by Richard Nixon to head up HEW. Reagan had a rare opportunity to handpick a man for an enormously powerful position—certainly a stepping stone to the governorship of California, if not the presidency. Reagan picked Congressman Ed Reinecke, who, Cannon reports, was taken completely by surprise. Reinecke had met Reagan only once, briefly, at a cocktail party. One would think that a committed free-market ideologue, as the president is painted to be by the media, would have at a minimum engaged a candidate for lieutenant governor in some in-depth interviews.

Whatever the reasons, it is safe to say that our political process in America today is not conducive to new ideas, despite the fact that the public is clearly searching for them. Gary Hart nearly won a nomination simply by *saying* he had new ideas. And just look at the response of our two lumbering political parties. The Democrats took off to a resort to contemplate new ideas with their star speaker Lee Iacocca, whose new idea was tried and found wanting in the thirties in Italy. And the Republicans boast Newt Gingrich, the ambitious young congressman from Georgia, whose new idea is to say yes to everything—a sort of "feel good politics," in which we can have tax cuts *and* major federal spending programs.

How can we rectify this situation? With utter disregard for what might be politically feasible, let me list a few suggestions. First, we should enact a major program of education tax credits or vouchers that would inject some sorely needed competition into our bureaucratic educational system. And here I'm not talking about $250 tax credits, which would help only those with children already in private schools, but credits of $1,500 or $1,800, which would allow lower- and middle-income parents to send their kids to decent private schools. We need a competition of ideas in order to generate interest in ideas.

Second, we should abolish the Federal Election Commission and bring back open competition to the political process. The more bureaucratized and rigidified the electoral process, the less we're going to have in the way of constructive new ideas. If voters want disclosure, they don't need an FEC to get it; they need only vote for candidates who offer it.

Third, the media need to take a more responsible attitude to elections. They should cover ideas and ignore fluff. When Gary Hart goes to Des Moines to pose with some cows, or Ronald Reagan goes to San Antonio to don a sombrero, they should go sans media. Those candidates willing to deal in substantive issues should receive substantive coverage. In this regard, I believe the technological revolution occurring in the telecommunications industry is a very healthy thing indeed: it is bringing true competition to the airwaves and stripping away the remaining vestiges of regulation and the quasi-official oligopoly of the networks, whose profoundly shallow coverage of political ideas can be attributed only to a lack of competition.

Fourth, we should consider a constitutional amendment that would limit representatives to three terms and senators to one term. There is actually a remarkable amount of support for such a proposal, as well there should be. When the Constitution was being debated, no one contemplated the phenomenon of the career legislator. The idea was that a representative from the community would take a couple of years off from his job, go to Washington for a while, and then return home. Nowadays, they stay in Washington even if they lose. Certainly, by limiting terms we can expect congressmen to be more interested in doing good rather than doing well. Power bases in Congress don't serve our nation's long-run interests, and congressmen intent on making a career in elected office are not likely to be intent on rocking the boat—or entertaining new ideas.

Finally, let me point out that there are plenty of interesting new policy ideas being set forth these days. We can safely say they are not coming from our political parties, and they tend not to come from polemical groups or even the larger established private institutions. Rather, there is a growing number of smaller think tanks and research organizations that are taking what I would call an entrepreneurial approach to public policy issues. In New York there is the Manhattan Institute, which has produced important works by George Gilder that have illuminated the important, indeed crucial, role of the entrepreneur in economic growth. More recently, the Manhattan Institute has published Charles Murray's brilliant new book *Losing Ground*, which, when both sides stop misinterpreting it, is destined to reshape our thinking on social welfare policy for decades to come.

In California, the Pacific Institute has just published an excellent new book on urban mass transit in which authors from across the political spectrum—or should I say "matrix"—make the case that it is precisely the absence of market constraints that has created a system that fails to move people efficiently and yet has an insatiable appetite for tax dollars.

In Montana, the Political Economy Research Center has undertaken truly innovative private-sector approaches to such issues as water rights, pollution, wilderness areas, timberlands, and other areas currently suffering from what we know as the "tragedy of the commons," which results from public ownership. Their New Resource Economics is gaining increasing recognition among intelligent environmentalists as an appropriate tool for dealing with environmental problems.

Finally, here at the Cato Institute we've been pleased with the reception to Peter Ferrara's proposal for a system of Super IRAs that would allow younger workers to partially opt out of Social Security, earn higher retirement income, and provide much-needed job-producing capital for our economy. I would also point to the contribution of our senior fellow Earl Ravenal in developing a methodology for analyzing the defense budget that emphasizes our foreign commitments rather than weapons systems or procurement systems. We point out that the vast majority of the military budget is designed to defend nations other than the United States. In NATO alone, for instance, we're spending some $130 billion this year—well over half our federal deficit—to defend Western European countries that collectively have more than twice the GNP of the Soviet-bloc countries (including the Soviet Union), superior technology, and a larger population. We question, under the circumstances, whether a phased withdrawal from NATO wouldn't save us significant amounts of money without endangering the security of Western Europe.

Government resistance to these and other new approaches to public policy is unfortunately almost reflexive. H. L. Mencken once wrote: "All [that government] can see in an original idea is potential change and hence, an invasion of its prerogatives. The most dangerous man, to any government, is the man who is able to think things out himself, without regard to the prevailing superstitions and taboos."

One such man is Nobel laureate F. A. Hayek, who wrote some time ago that we must "make the philosophic foundations of a free society once more a living intellectual issue, and its implementation a task which challenges the ingenuity and imagination of our liveliest minds." There are numerous interesting new policy options available these days that are consistent with the traditional American values of peace, limited government, and a respect for individual rights. Given the reforms I've outlined above, I believe they could and should be an important part of political debate in America.

Paul D. Kleppner:* Speaking in March to the 12th annual Conservative Political Action Conference, President Reagan affirmed the triumph of conservative values, which he said had occurred "because the other side is virtually bankrupt of ideas; it has nothing more to say, nothing to add to the debate." Conservatives have "captured the moment, captured the imagination of the American people," Mr. Reagan continued, "because we are winning the contest of ideas."[1]

Of course, not everyone reads recent events, and especially the 1984 election results, in this light. As in 1980, many of those who voted for Mr. Reagan last November did so despite disagreeing with one or more of his positions on economic, social, or foreign policy issues.[2] Citizens with differing opinions contributed to his winning coalition, including those whose views were anchored in the opposite extremes on such matters as abortion and control of nuclear weapons. From this perspective, the election was a massive personal victory reflecting the general public's sense that economic conditions were better than they had been in 1980, that "it's morning again in America." As Texas commissioner of agriculture Jim Hightower observed, explaining his party's resounding defeat, "There is no right or left, there is only what works."[3]

Which claim should we believe? Are ideas, especially the ideas of conservatives, the force driving the reorganization of voting coalitions and the redirection of public policy that we are now experiencing? Are these ideas like the locomotive of a train, pulling the general public into a "golden age of freedom," as President Reagan suggested? Or, as Commissioner Hightower's explanation implies, have ideas become more like the caboose of a freight train, decorative ornaments whose only remaining purpose is to evoke memories of bygone days?

The answer may seem painfully apparent. If the general public lacks coherent sets of beliefs bearing on public policy, its collective

---

*The author entitled his talk "Leaders, Voters, and Ideas: A View of Changing Relationships."

[1]Quoted in the *Washington Post*, March 2, 1985.

[2]See the reports on the CBS/*New York Times* exit polls in the *New York Times*, November 9, 1980 and November 11, 1984. Also see NBC News, Inc., *Decision 1984: General Election Poll Results*.

[3]Quoted in *Mother Jones* 10 (February/March 1985): 8.

voting choice could hardly signal the ascendancy of conservative ideas or any other type of ideas, for that matter. Under these circumstances, we might expect elections to pivot on assessments of the personal characteristics of the candidates or on a generalized sense of the "goodness" or "badness" of current economic conditions; but we couldn't read the results as conveying any policy mandates, any clear guidelines for future action. If such is indeed the case, then Commissioner Hightower's assessment would be accurate, and President Reagan's judgment would be wishful thinking.

But we cannot lay the matter to rest so easily, for the role of ideas in American politics has never been as simple as these conflicting judgments presume. To assess their role we need to take two additional factors into account. First, ideas operate in distinctive ways at different levels of society, and the key task that faces political leaders is to link these separate levels of understanding together. Second, the task of connecting different levels of political understanding has itself become much more complex and difficult over time, largely because changes in the economy, in communications, in transportation, in organizational technologies, and in the extent and level of education have fundamentally altered how citizens relate themselves to the larger world that lies beyond their personal experience.

How do people understand politics? How do they explain to themselves the wide array of public policies in which governments engage? How do they pick and choose among the sometimes ambiguous and always contradictory evaluations of these policies? Their cognitive task would be formidable if the human mind simply piled one shapeless experience on top of the other. Fortunately, it operates in a relational fashion, enabling humans to view "new" experiences through interpretive frameworks reflecting their old values and past experiences. The capacity of the human mind to develop this sort of relational framework, or perspective, enables individuals to interpret new stimuli, to give order and meaning to the "great, blooming, buzzing confusion" in the world about them.[4]

---

[4]The following works have been especially useful in developing this understanding of cognitive processes and belief systems: Howard P. Becker, *Through Values to Social Interpretation: Essays on Social Contexts, Actions, Types and Prospects* (Westport, Conn.: Greenwood Press, 1968); Ludwig Landgrebe, "The World as a Phenomenological Problem," *Philosophy and Phenomenological Research* 1 (September 1940): 35–

But it also means that particular events and statements will be perceived differently, depending on the experiences and values of those doing the interpreting. This follows from the simple reality that human experience is limited rather than universal, thus giving rise to limited, not universal, patterns of thought and behavior. Each individual or group has a particular situation in society, with a distinctive consciousness of the world, distinctive values and goals, which are understandable in terms of that situation. Their knowledge of the world is limited by the extent of the world with which they have had experience.

For example, the person whose consciousness of the world derives from experiences in a local community from which he does not move physically or psychologically has a limited perspective and consequently a circumscribed pattern of values and behavior. Those whose outlooks are shaped by involvement in geographically wider but still socially homogeneous patterns of association have broader but still limited perspectives. And those whose contacts and experiences are both broader geographically and more varied socially develop yet other, although still limited, patterns of thought. The assembly-line worker views the world differently from the corporation's executive officers, the Nebraska farmer differently from the grain exporter, the black ghetto resident differently from the black suburban dweller, the Catholic from the Protestant or Jew, the older Polish immigrant from the newer Puerto Rican, the New Englander from the Southerner—because their values, past experiences, and present circumstances are different, and these characteristics peculiarly shape the contexts in which their perspectives develop.[5]

Thus, no simple answer can be given to the basic question of how people interpret and explain political events and actions to themselves. We can only develop a series of responses, each dealing with *particular* people, occupying *particular* situations in society, and bringing *particular* perspectives to bear on the process. Or, to put it more succinctly, and as an adage that gained popularity in

---

58; Karl Mannheim, *Ideology and Utopia: An Introduction to the Sociology of Knowledge* (New York: Harcourt Brace Jovanovich, 1955); Milton Rokeach, *Beliefs, Attitudes, and Values: A Theory of Organization and Change* (San Francisco: Jossey-Bass, 1968) and idem, *The Open and Closed Mind: Investigations into the Nature of Belief Systems and Personality Systems* (New York: Basic Books, 1960).

[5]See the discussion in Samuel P. Hays, "Situational Analysis," in *American Political History as Social Analysis* (Knoxville: University of Tennessee Press, 1980), pp. 104–9.

Machiavelli's time expressed it, "The thought of the palace is one thing, . . . that of the public square is another."[6]

Rephrasing this Renaissance expression in terms more appropriate to the American context, we can say that there is a wide gap between the perspectives that political activists develop and those that typically characterize other segments of the general public. Probably such has always been the case, with those interested and willing to devote their time and energy to political activities being better informed and more supportive of their party's positions on issues than citizens for whom campaigns and elections are only seasonal affairs.

Since the 1960s, however, the size of this gap between leaders and followers has increased enormously. Jeane Kirkpatrick documented an important stage of this development by showing the large distance between the ideological orientation of the Democratic party's identifiers among the general public and the party's delegates to its 1972 national convention.[7] More recent evidence shows a similar gap between these two Democratic groupings in 1976 and 1980. However, this evidence also shows that an equally large ideological gap has emerged between Republican leaders and identifiers, with that party's convention delegates in 1976 and 1980 showing a much higher level of ideological constraint than earlier. Unlike 1972, when Nixon's delegates were an ideologically diverse group, the delegates who represented Reagan in 1980 (and presumably in 1984 as well) were as ideologically pure and as ideologically distant from their party's rank and file as McGovern's supporters had been in 1972.[8]

While this description applies to only one level of political activity, other evidence and observation suggest comparable developments elsewhere, especially in the House of Representatives and in the selection of candidates for statewide offices. In addition, the last two decades have witnessed the emergence of several ideologically focused organizations, nationwide in scope and most of them con-

[6]Mannheim, p. 63.

[7]Jeane Kirkpatrick, *The New Presidential Elite: Men and Women in National Politics* (New York: Russell Sage Foundation, 1976).

[8]Barbara G. Farah, M. Kent Jennings, and Warren E. Miller, "Convention Delegates: Reform and the Representation of Party Elites, 1972–1980," paper presented at the Conference on Presidential Activities, College of William and Mary, Williamsburg, Va., October 1981.

servative in orientation. These organizations are capable of enlisting local opinion leaders, bringing them into contact with each other as well as with middle- and upper-level leaders, providing each level an open channel for communicating with the others and thus cementing commitments based on shared sets of values and beliefs. Clearly, among persons operating at these levels of political activity, ideas predominate as organizing and motivating forces.

In all likelihood, it was these types of developments that President Reagan had in mind when he proclaimed victory in the "contest of ideas." There is clear evidence of ideological thinking on the part of conservative activists, and their ranks are larger, and their organizations more energetic, than ever before. As a result, conservative thought now dominates the political scene at this level of action. It now defines the terms, establishes the boundaries, and sets the agenda for the debate over public policy.

Despite this dominance by conservative activists, however, the battle for ideological hegemony has not yet been won, and, under contemporary conditions, it may not be winnable. The final victory to which the president alluded still awaits the resolution of another problem: How do the few communicate their conviction to the many? How do activists communicate their vision of what ought to be to citizens with different and more limited perspectives? How does unity of purpose emerge from this diversity of outlook?

Political activists have traditionally sought to mobilize broader public support for their vision by taking "the roles of the publics whose support they need." They design their actions, speeches, and postures to make them significant symbols, evoking "common meaning" for both their audiences and themselves. In this way, their targeted publics become reassured that the activists "represent" them, at least symbolically.[9] The coalition that results is not held together by ideological cement, but by a psychological rapport focusing on shared values.

Of course, activists are not free to say whatever particular publics want to hear. They are limited by their visions of what ought to be. But within that context, they search for and attempt to mobilize support among groups that share at least some of their values and identify with at least some common symbols. In the process, they employ the central elements from their own belief systems as highly

9Murray Edelman, *The Symbolic Uses of Politics* (Urbana: University of Illinois Press, 1967), p. 188.

simplified code words, or catch phrases, to evoke common meaning with their targeted publics.

Consider some past examples of how the process operates. In the 1850s, the activists who built the Republican coalition articulated anti-party and anti-Southern themes to and for groups whose political outlooks had already been conditioned by involvement in the antislavery, temperance, and/or anti-Catholic crusades of the 1840s and 1850s. Attacks on the "Spirit of Party" reminded these groups of their shared belief that only an "all-absorbing party spirit" had prevented them from succeeding.[10] Denunciations of slavery and of the aggressive spirit of the "Slave Power" reminded these groups of their sectional enemy, but their reference wasn't limited to the South's labor system. Consistent with their evangelical values, these groups regarded anything that obstructed the operation of man's free will—his right to do right, in the common expression of that time—as a peril to his and to society's salvation. All such restraints were sinful forms of slavery. Christians, charged with doing God's work, were required to purge all sin from their society, whether the bondage of the black to his white owner, or the immigrant to the dictates of the pope, or any man to the influence of King Alcohol or to the Spirit of Party.[11]

Of course, not every antislavery man was also anti-Catholic, nor was every anti-Catholic crusader a supporter of temperance, nor were all equally repulsed by the "Spirit of Party" and the "Slave Power." But there was a broad consonance based on common religious values, and the anti-party and anti-Southern themes became the least common denominators expressing that shared psychological rapport. In a sense, the "thought of the palace" was simplified into code words that caught the attention, and evoked the emotional commitment, of those who mingled in "the public square."

The Democratic party's activists of the period also distilled their belief systems into code words and phrases to evoke common meaning between themselves and their targeted support groups. By the 1880s, they concentrated on portraying their party as the defender of "personal liberty." Linked with the party's regular denunciations of prohibition and Sunday-closing laws, the per-

[10]*Boston Daily Advertiser*, November 11, 1844; [Neil Dow], *The Reminiscences of Neil Dow, Recollections of Eighty Years* (Portland, Me., 1898), pp. 446–49.

[11]Paul Kleppner, *The Third Electoral System, 1853–1892: Parties, Voters, and Political Cultures* (Chapel Hill: University of North Carolina Press, 1979), pp. 60–74.

sonal-liberty theme reminded such groups as the German Luther-
ans and the Catholics of the Democratic party's commitment to
laissez-faire ethics, to the proposition "that it is not the legitimate
province of government to control the habits, tastes, appetites, and
liberties of the people." At the same time, the theme reminded
Catholic voters of the actions of Democratic state officeholders in
supporting freedom-of-worship measures and opposing laws that
aimed at closing parochial schools. Linked with the party's defense
of states' rights and its opposition to the centralization of power at
the federal level, the theme appealed to the party's Southern constituency. It reminded them that the Democratic party defended
their freedom from all intrusions by officers of the federal government, especially interferences in the conduct of elections.[12]

The critical point is that these themes, and others that could be
used as examples from different historical periods, were not simply
empty campaign slogans. They were phrases expressing in simplified form the more elaborate belief systems that motivated the
behavior of each party's activists. Properly understood, these code
words and phrases aptly and adequately captured those "common
meanings" that bridged the gap between activists and the general
public, surmounted diverse perspectives deriving from distinct geographic and social situations, and united each party's supporters
into a purposive coalition. Moreover, since the belief systems that
these themes expressed guided the behavior of each party's activists
in shaping public policy, they succinctly summarized the essence
of the contrast in the political characters of the major parties. In
those days, "Democrat" symbolized a commitment to a culturally
diverse society and to an active, restricted government that would
guarantee "the largest liberty consistent with public welfare."[13]
"Republican," on the other hand, symbolized the evangelical drive
for cultural homogenization and a commitment to an active federal
government that intruded into both the economic and social relations of its citizens.

Needless to say, the actions and auras of the major parties have
changed drastically since the late nineteenth century. But one can
make a compelling case that the political activists of the 1980s are

[12]The quotation is from the 1882 Democratic platform in Illinois, in *Appletons'
Annual Cyclopaedia and Register of Important Events of the Year 1882* (New York, 1882),
p. 385.

[13]Ohio Democratic platform 1882, in ibid., p. 659.

still doing what their predecessors did: distilling their belief systems into verbal and visual symbols designed to evoke common meaning among a general public with more limited perspectives. However, and quite obviously, these actions don't have the same effect now as they did in earlier eras. What is glaringly absent from the contemporary scene is the kind of tidy unity that cut across diverse situations and levels of political activity in bygone days. Instead, what we are witnessing is a strong tendency toward ideological homogenization among the activists within each party, which leads to a sharper ideological polarization between the parties. Paradoxically, however, this process had led to an increase, rather than a decrease, in the ideological distance between each party's activist cadre and its supporters among the general public. Unlike their earlier counterparts, and despite clearly superior technologies and organizational infrastructures at their disposal, the political activists of our time seem unable to communicate persuasively with the many who are not already true believers.

This deficiency does not reflect a lack of commitment, energy, or even money. It derives from the changes society has undergone over the past four decades, in which old institutions and structures have been rendered obsolete but have not yet been replaced with new ones through which citizens with limited perspectives can understand the political world that lies beyond their personal experience.

In the nineteenth century, and even earlier in this one, prevailing social conditions reinforced the process of symbolic linkage between political activists and the general public. It was a simpler world, one characterized by relatively low levels of interdependence and flows of information. It was always a polyglot society, but one in which people tended to deploy themselves into well-bounded "island communities," psychologically if not physically, isolated from each other. It was a world of close ties, of what Peter Berger and John Neuhaus have called "mediating structures"—neighborhood, family, church, and voluntary associations.[14] It was through their

<hr />

[14]Peter L. Berger and Richard John Neuhaus, *To Empower People: The Role of Mediating Structures in Public Policy* (Washington: American Enterprise Institute, 1977). The concept of "island communities" is from Robert H. Wiebe, *The Search for Order, 1877–1920* (Westport, Conn.: Greenwood Press, 1980), especially pp. 11–44. The concept's applicability even to later twentieth century contexts is shown in Herbert J. Gans, *The Urban Villagers: Group and Class in the Life of Italian Americans* (New York: Free Press, 1965), pp. 3–41, 142–226.

involvement in networks centered on these organizations that most people related themselves to the larger world beyond their personal experience. Moreover, it was from these networks of social relations that each party's political activists emerged, and through them that these rising leaders continued to communicate with their supportive publics. Finally, when they did the communicating, political activists virtually controlled the flow of political information: over three-quarters of the country's daily and weekly newspapers were partisan organs. Under these conditions, the processes of political communication and socialization operated effectively, party coalitions were unified and remarkably stable, interest in political matters was widespread, and, as a consequence, participation rates reached their historic high points.[15]

Especially since World War II, human life and experience have been reorganized, altering these older relationships among citizens, activists, and political ideas. Family and community life, work, and leisure activities have changed drastically over the past 40 years. The context of family life has changed from one dominated by a norm of mutual cooperation aimed at collective family goals to a norm fostering the creative development of individual family members. Postwar gains in real income and living standards made it possible for people to devote more time and energy to this new mode of family life and its associated leisure activities, at the expense of work-related involvements. The postwar automobile and road-building booms inaugurated massive suburbanization, a migration from city to suburbs that focused primarily on the family as a unit and operated to further privatize family life and to sharpen the distinction between it and work experiences. The new patterns of life resulting from these changes increasingly separated the spheres of personal experience, thus breaking down the linkages among family, community, work, church, and voluntary associations that earlier supported the operation of political communication and socialization processes.[16] The networks of social relations in which people became involved no longer centered so exclusively on the traditional mediating structures, with the consequence that these

<hr />

[15]Peter R. Knights, " 'Competition' in the U.S. Daily Newspaper Industry, 1865–68," *Journalism Quarterly* 45 (Autumn 1968): 473–80.

[16]Hays, pp. 246–47; and idem, "Politics and Society: Beyond the Political Party," in Paul Kleppner et al., *The Evolution of American Electoral Systems* (Westport, Conn.: Greenwood Press, 1981), pp. 243–68.

institutions ceased to offer activists a channel for communicating with their public. As the capacity of the traditional mediating institutions declined, most citizens were left on their own to develop new norms for understanding politics, to seek new ways of explaining how events beyond their experience became relevant to their personal lives.

Other postwar changes made this search for understanding even more difficult. Since the late 1940s, life has become increasingly enmeshed in large-scale systems of control that are centrally directed and managed. These modern technical systems, embodying the spirit of science and empirical inquiry, came to touch virtually all aspects of human life—the economy, education, government, religion—and every phase of human experience came to involve participation in one or another of these systems.[17] The growth of these massive institutional systems, both private and public, reshaped the context within which public affairs subsequently evolved. Their penetrative capability shifted much of the rule making that touched people's lives from elected to administrative bodies and in the process altered the terms of political discourse, so that issues were increasingly articulated in the language of technocratic experts. All of this made much of the world of public affairs seem increasingly complex and difficult to understand, especially to citizens who at the same time were being cut off from the mediating structures they had traditionally relied on for political interpretation and cues.

In a society where change is the only constant, and where the old mediating structures no longer effectively relate individuals to the larger political world, we might expect politics to devolve into a Hobbesian "war of all against all." Some people point to the proliferation of special-interest groups and political action committees, to the decline of political parties, to the steep drop in voter turnout since 1960, and to other such symptoms as indicating that this war is already in progress.[18] I am not so pessimistic as to suggest that such an outcome is inevitable.

It is true that political life in this country has been fundamentally transformed since World War II, and analysts are still groping for

[17]Hays, "Politics and Society," pp. 263–65. For the effect of these developments on the electoral system, see Paul Kleppner, Who Voted? The Dynamics of Electoral Turnout, 1870–1980 (New York: Praeger, 1982), pp. 112–41.

[18]For example, see Morris P. Fiorina, "The Decline of Collective Responsibility in American Politics," Daedalus 109 (Summer 1980): 25–46.

categories that describe and explain the results. We know at least, as Professors Maddox and Lilie have convincingly shown, that the old liberal-conservative dichotomy no longer adequately captures the range of public thought, if it ever did. Instead, they suggest using two issue dimensions—government economic intervention and expansion of personal freedoms—to divide the public into four ideological categories: liberal, conservative, libertarian, and populist.[19] While this scheme better depicts the real world and is analytically useful for some purposes, important aspects of contemporary political thought still elude it.

It seems to me that postwar politics have been dominated by two major characteristics. The first is yet another of those politico-moral movements that have been periodically recurring features of American politics. The second, more important though virtually unnoticed, involves a powerful tendency toward political specialization.

Because the United States is the kind of society it is, with the kind of history it has had, conflicts over modernizing change have always tended to be viewed and expressed in moralistic terms. Thus, even when it has not been the central focus of political discourse, pietistic moralism has remained a brooding presence lurking barely beneath the surface.[20] Now it has burst forth once again in the form of a highly politicized revitalization movement, the so-called Religious Right.

This latest wave of religious enthusiasm is clearly a response to the reorganization of life and the reorientation of personal experience during the postwar years. These changes unmistakably undermined traditional values, and public actions and events seemed only to confirm this falling away from "the straight and narrow." Supreme Court decisions in school prayer and abortion cases, the gay rights and feminist movements, skyrocketing divorce rates—all of these and other indicators suggest to some a society broken loose from its moral foundations. Those who perceive these developments as threats to their values have resorted to revitalization strategies. And these strategies now, as they always have in the

[19]William S. Maddox and Stuart A. Lilie, *Beyond Liberal and Conservative: Reassessing the Political Spectrum* (Washington: Cato Institute, 1984), pp. 4–20.

[20]This is the focus of Walter Dean Burnham, "The 1980 Earthquake: Realignment, Reaction, or What?" in *The Hidden Election: Politics and Economics in the 1980 Presidential Campaign,* ed. Thomas Ferguson and Joel Rogers (New York: Pantheon, 1981), pp. 98–140. Also see Paul Kleppner, "Piety, Federalism, and the Shaping of U.S. Politics," *Mid-Stream* 22 (July/October 1983): 400–418.

past, rely heavily on using the power of government to coerce compliance with their notion of righteous behavior.

Certainly, the Religious Right has captured the attention of the media, and the movement may even win some legislative and judicial victories in the short run. But its success is likely to be fleeting because the movement swims against the tide of social and attitudinal change, tilts at the wrong windmills, and offers an inappropriate solution—public coercion rather than private conversion.

The second characteristic of the postwar years, the tendency toward political specialization, is by far the more important because it is likely to be the more durable. Unlike the revitalization of the Religious Right, this tendency reflects, rather than counterattacks, the social and attitudinal changes of the last forty years. Those changes have worked to separate the spheres of personal experience and to alter the context and terms of political discourse, making the latter more technical, complex, and difficult for people to relate to their own lives. The tendency for people to specialize, to pick and choose among policy areas of concern and knowledge, rather than to evince an interest in politics in general, represents a reasonable and rational response to these altered conditions.

Unfortunately, most public opinion polls miss this tendency toward political specialization because they ask simply whether citizens favor or oppose some issue, and sometimes whether the respondent's interest in that issue is high, low, or nonexistent. But they do not usually inquire into what the respondent knows about the issue or how this information was acquired. Thus, we usually cannot distinguish responses reflecting high interest and information from the ones that may be only intuitive, on-the-spot choices from among the articulated options. Yet, clearly, these are responses of different kinds, representing wholly different orientations to the world of public affairs.

Fortunately, two national surveys did ask the questions that make these sorts of distinctions possible. The first was the 1978 National Public Affairs Study, a clustered probability sample of approximately 4,200 high school and college students. The second was a 1979 survey of over 1,600 adults, which was designed in part to repeat the earlier year's questions concerning interest in and information about various issue areas.[21] The findings of these studies

[21]The 1978 NPAS study was conducted under a grant from the National Science Foundation. The technical details of the sample characteristics, data-collection pro-

are rich in detail, and together they help us to better understand how people have chosen to relate themselves to the increasingly complex world of public affairs.

Briefly, both studies point to a two-step process. At the first stage, citizens decide whether or not to devote the time and resources necessary to pay attention to politics. This choice is not easy for most citizens, given the alternative demands on their time, the high costs associated with acquiring increasingly technical information, and the fact that the allocation of time is always a zero-sum situation. As a result, only a minority of the sampled populations placed a high priority on keeping up-to-date on political affairs or on influencing political events. As we might have anticipated, a lower proportion of the young adults—only 39 percent—gave politics this priority, while 49 percent of the older citizens viewed politics as a salient area, with the proportion reaching nearly three-fifths among those between 35 and 54 years of age.

The second step in the process is the more significant because it affects the minorities for whom politics is a subject of interest and concern. At this stage both the young adults and their older counterparts behaved similarly: each elected to specialize, limiting their interest to a small number of issues while remaining unconcerned and generally uninformed about other areas of public policy.[22] Among the young adults for whom politics was salient, 39 percent expressed interest in a single issue, and an additional 30 percent showed interest in two issues. There was only slightly less specialization among older adults, with 48 percent of those for whom politics was salient narrowing their interest to as few as two issue areas. And neither young nor older adults chose their areas of interest randomly or in response to the mass media's focus of attention. Their choices related to their own career interests, educational backgrounds or expectations, and, in the case of older adults, to their

cedures, and questionnaire are reported in Jon D. Miller, Robert Suchner, and Alan Voelker, *Citizenship in an Age of Science* (New York: Pergamon, 1980), chap. 4. The 1979 survey was supported by the Science Indicators Unit of the National Science Foundation. A full description of the technical information may be found in Jon D. Miller, Kenneth Prewitt, and Robert Pearson, *The Attitudes of the U.S. Public Toward Science and Technology*, report of the National Opinion Research Center to the National Science Foundation, 1980.

[22]Jon D. Miller, "Political Specialization: A Behavioral Imperative," paper presented at the annual meeting of the American Political Science Association, Washington, August 1980.

current occupations. Moreover, this type of specialization involved more than passing interest: these citizens, young and old alike, actively pursued information relevant to their areas of concern, reading about the topic not only in newspapers and general circulation magazines, but in specialized and technical sources as well. Such citizens constitute the core of an attentive public; however, unlike their ancestors, they have no affinity for politics in general but an informed interest in only a limited number of issue areas.

To those who believe that citizens should be knowledgeable about all or most issues, this must appear to be a dire and dangerous development. To those who strive to reduce the varieties of political thinking to some limited number of categories, this tendency toward specialization will prove frustratingly elusive. But it represents a wholly rational response to a world beyond personal experience, a world where political issues are increasingly cast in technical terms, where the costs of acquiring information are correspondingly high, and where the competing demands on time are great. Moreover, political specialization among the general public should not be viewed simply as a threat to our political system. To the contrary, the involvement of narrowly but actively interested and better-informed citizens can only enrich the process.

But this development does pose a new order of challenge to the remaining political generalists, those who yearn for coalitions glued together by shared values and commitments. They must now face the twin tasks of evoking common meaning among interested and informed specialists, the people least likely to be moved by vague symbols, and of developing new mediating structures capable of penetrating to the grass roots of society. Whether they can win this part of the "contest of ideas" under current conditions is at best an open question. But if it is unwinnable, then we face a protracted period of shifting coalitions, alternating landslides, and abrupt zigs and zags in the direction of public policy. This may be unsettling, even discomforting, to those who expect orderly transformations followed by short periods of consolidation and longer ones of stability. However, even in this outcome, which is by no means assured, there is little cause for pessimism or loss of confidence. Our political system has successfully weathered much worse, including major depressions and a Civil War. Indeed, it is the genius of our political arrangements to be resilient enough to withstand our best, or our worst, efforts to shatter them.

John Barnes, Evans and Novak: *I agree with Mr. Crane that we'd be better off without the FEC, but I wonder how his idea of getting rid of the FEC and giving the voter the choice of not voting for someone who won't disclose squares with the idea of limiting our representatives to three terms and our senators to one. Doesn't that fly in the face of giving the voter the widest possible choice of representation?*

Crane: I'm actually being generous in my proposal. I'd like to limit congressmen to one term as well, and limit all congressional terms to a couple of months each. We're talking about a political system that has coercive power over our lives. We need constitutional constraints that are intelligently designed to limit the power of government, such as a balanced-budget amendment or limits on the terms of congressmen. It's just ludicrous to suggest that a congressional district of 500,000 people has only one person who is qualified to represent it for over 20 years. The build-up of political power and patronage over multi-term periods is counterproductive to the interests of the American people. And that's why I'm against it.

Contributors

Lee Atwater, former deputy director of the Reagan-Bush '84 Committee, is a political consultant with Black, Manafort, Stone & Atwater.

Michael Barone, a senior editorial writer for the *Washington Post,* is also coauthor of *The Almanac of American Politics.*

David Boaz, vice president of the Cato Institute, is co-editor of *Beyond the Status Quo: Policy Proposals for America.*

Pat Caddell is president of Cambridge Survey Research and has worked as a pollster for George McGovern, Jimmy Carter, and Gary Hart.

Terry Nichols Clark is a professor of sociology at the University of Chicago, senior study director at the National Opinion Research Center, and coauthor of *City Money: Political Processes, Fiscal Strain and Retrenchment.*

Edward H. Crane, president of the Cato Institute, is co-editor of *Beyond the Status Quo: Policy Proposals for America.*

Mervin Field is chairman of the Field Research Corporation and directs the California Poll.

Paul D. Kleppner is presidential research professor of history and political science and director of the Social Science Research Institute at Northern Illinois University. His books include *The Cross of Culture* and *Chicago Divided: The Making of a Black Mayor.*

Stuart A. Lilie, associate professor of political science at the University of Central Florida, is coauthor of *Beyond Liberal and Conservative: Reassessing the Political Spectrum.*

Dotty Lynch, political editor of CBS News, formerly headed Lynch Research and served as chief pollster for Gary Hart's 1984 presidential campaign.

William S. Maddox is coauthor of *Beyond Liberal and Conservative: Reassessing the Political Spectrum*.

William Schneider is a resident fellow at the American Enterprise Institute, contributing editor to *National Journal* and the *Los Angeles Times*, and coauthor of a forthcoming book, *The Radical Center: New Directions in American Politics*.

Paul H. Weaver, former assistant managing editor of *Fortune* magazine, is editor and publisher of *The Fed Fortnightly* and author of a forthcoming book, *The End of the Corporate State*.

Vin Weber is a Republican congressman from Minnesota and a leader of the Conservative Opportunity Society.

Tim Wirth is a Democratic congressman from Colorado and chairman of the subcommittee on telecommunications.

Cato Institute

Founded in 1977, the Cato Institute is a public policy research foundation dedicated to broadening the parameters of policy debate to allow consideration of more options that are consistent with the traditional American principles of limited government, individual liberty, and peace. Toward that goal, the Institute strives to achieve a greater involvement of the intelligent, concerned lay public in questions of policy and the proper role of government.

The Institute is named for *Cato's Letters*, pamphlets that were widely read in the American Colonies in the early eighteenth century and played a major role in laying the philosophical foundation for the revolution that followed. Since that revolution, civil and economic liberties have been eroded as the number and complexity of social problems have grown. Today virtually no aspect of human life is free from the domination of a governing class of politico-economic interests. A pervasive intolerance for individual rights is shown by government's arbitrary intrusions into private economic transactions and its disregard for civil liberties.

To counter this trend the Cato Institute undertakes an extensive publications program dealing with the complete spectrum of policy issues. Books, monographs, and shorter studies are commissioned to examine the federal budget, Social Security, regulation, NATO, international trade, and a myriad of other issues. Major policy conferences are held throughout the year, from which papers are published thrice yearly in the *Cato Journal*.

In order to maintain an independent posture, the Cato Institute accepts no government funding. Contributions are received from foundations, corporations, and individuals, and other revenue is generated from the sale of publications. The Institute is a nonprofit, tax-exempt, educational foundation under Section 501(c)3 of the Internal Revenue Code.

CATO INSTITUTE
224 Second St., S.E.
Washington, D.C. 20003